# CHAOS TO CALM

CLEANING AND ORGANIZING WITH ADHD

ABIGAIL SHEPARD

# CONTENTS

# INTRODUCTION

Have you ever placed something super important, like a passport or your next utility bill, in a safe spot, somewhere more organized and cleaner, only to go and forget that safe spot within the next couple of hours? Because I have, too. I know firsthand how stressful the process of searching and scanning every corner of your house is, looking with desperation to find that item. Usually, I'm in a rush to find it, too, often late for an appointment, meeting, or even a work presentation. Sometimes, it can feel as though tidying my house or even my room is equivalent to taming a tornado.

So, when it comes to keeping those important items safe, that overwhelming feeling creeps into my head, assuming control over my entire body. This usually causes my ADHD brain to spiral into a whirlwind of confusion and procrastination, believing that a safe spot is the best option for this crucial object when I can barely remember that that trusted location even exists. This repetitive cycle became tiresome. I was sick of convincing myself that this was just who I was, being portrayed as forgetful and messy by neurotypical people. From that moment on, a journey began, one that involved taking back control from all the chaos and clutter and redefining my neurodivergent self as capable and resilient. I invite you to take this journey with me to not only learn more about the world of organization but to change your reality and, ultimately, to regain control over your life and surroundings.

I think we all can agree that a huge benefit to having a clean home is the aesthetics. It is like candy to a child; it looks beautiful, and the taste of achievement is even better! But what if I told you that a clean home isn't just beneficial because it's visually pleasing? An organized environment has an array of benefits ranging from physical, psychological, and even financial. Our environment plays an influential role that is key to a successful and righteous well-being.

One of the many advantages of keeping an organized home is improved health, which is crucial for a long and enjoyable life. When we are unorganized and generally messy, the vast majority of us have the tendency to ignore the consequences it can have on our health. For instance, have you ever noticed that nasty cold that keeps recurring or those itchy eyes and runny nose symptoms that just won't stop pestering you? This could be due to a build-up of pollen, mold, and even pet hair for those who own furry friends. A lack of cleaning can easily cause allergy symptoms as well as decrease your air quality. Subsequently, this causes labored breathing, leaving you tired and possibly in the emergency room. The solution to this is regularly vacuuming, wiping surfaces, and mopping, which can feel like a daunting experience to some of us. Thus, within this book, we will discuss different strategies to make these tasks less daunting. For instance, adopting cleaning routines where we break down the big tasks into small chunks. Remember, cleaning does not need to be perfect to reap the rewards.

A common metaphor is that we are a product of our environment; this means that we inevitably become our habits, emotions, and what we surround ourselves with. For instance, when we surround ourselves with a messy home, we are subconsciously adding stress and chaos that we could have prevented, ultimately leading to a disorientated mind. Scientists have found that increased mess in our homes can trigger the release of cortisol, the "stress hormone." Cortisol is usually associated with situations that trigger our fight or flight, helping us to perform at our best in scary situations. However, it is also the hormone responsible for managing the circadian cycle, otherwise known as our sleep cycle. This means it's essential that we allow for a high release of cortisol in the morning and manage a steady decrease during the day to have a healthy sleep at night. Thus, keeping a tidy bedroom is paramount for not only a good night's sleep but also productivity and mental clarity.

Furthermore, the thought of cleaning an unorganized house that might not have been touched or cleaned for months or even years can feel debilitating. Reaching out for help from friends and family can feel shameful and embarrassing, making it a burden that usually only lies on one person's shoulders. The combination of humiliation, embarrassment, and fear of inviting people over or engaging in social activities can cause your self-esteem to plummet. Low self-esteem is usually accompanied by depression, so it's important to note that your mess does not define you as a person. Seeking help from family, friends, or other resources is an incredibly brave step toward growth and self-improvement.

At one point in our lives, most of us have said that we don't have enough time for something, whether spending time with loved ones or even going to the gym; not having enough time is a universal feeling. While decluttering can be overwhelming, having and maintaining an organized home is one way to slow down the clock. Different organizational approaches, like minimalism, make life abundantly easier. It means that things you need become easily accessible, and cleaning will become far quicker due to minimal clutter being in your way. It also reduces overstimulation in neurodivergent people who suffer from sensory issues. So, the next time you wish to take a nap or a relaxing bath, you'll be able to kick back and unwind now that you have removed clutter and eliminated overstimulation, allowing for mental clarity.

By making these changes in your home, you'll not only benefit mentally and physically but also financially. If we consider an improved sleep cycle, mental clarity, and enhanced health while reducing cortisol levels and creating more time for ourselves, this opens the door to more financial freedom. Those groceries that were left at the back of your fridge untouched because you couldn't find them have finally become fresh ingredients for a meal that is eaten and not wasted. Those tennis balls or that pair of sunglasses you bought again because you thought you lost them are now stored exactly where they should be. This means that you'll no longer be wasting money on repurposing items you believed to have lost or couldn't find. Instead, you'll be saving or spending it on something that fulfills you far more than mere consumerism.

As adults, we are expected to know how to do everything. The more years we spend on earth, the higher the expectations are, the more knowledge we should have, and the more skills we should have acquired. But sometimes, we have absolutely no idea where to even begin, and that is okay. Many of us don't know how to clean and organize our living spaces, and having an ADHD brain can make this feel like climbing Mount Everest without ever having stepped on a treadmill. Plus, if you have ADHD, I'm sure you've experienced the feeling that everything needs to be perfect before you begin a task or finish one. Perfectionism is usually an unhealthy coping mechanism for those who dealt with excessive criticism growing up. Focusing on a certain thing until it is perfect would essentially prove the critics wrong. It's so important to remember that perfection is not the required outcome, nor is it the goal of organizing your home.

There are a few ways to combat those thoughts that tell you perfection is the only acceptable result. This includes redefining your expectations, which means taking things slowly and separating tasks into manageable chunks instead of over-bearing chaos that will consume your attention for that week. For example, on day one, you could start by allocating items to their designated room. Within the next few days, begin organizing those items in each room, like placing the pans in a cupboard near the stove. This tiny change revolutionizes your kitchen into a functional space. Furthermore, there are people who want to help you, reach out to family and friends, or even hire a personal organizer if you have the means. Not to mention, there are support groups at the tip of your fingers, and places like Facebook and Reddit have groups and forums where others share their experiences with ADHD and a messy home. It's a great outlet for days when your doom pile has suddenly grown.

Just like a racing river, our thoughts and impulses are fast-flowing, using torrents of energy that carve a messy path. To create calmness, you must build levees and channels or harness strategies and routines that guide the river's energy in a controlled and productive direction. Trust the exhausting process, and you will unveil a blissful reality you thought you'd never achieve. Take my hand on this journey, and step by step, we will unravel coping techniques and strategies that will guide us to an improved way of living. Embarking on this journey means you will gain valuable insight on how to conquer your ADHD symptoms. Additionally, you will learn how to harness the power of your ADHD mindset and use it to boost productivity, eliminate clutter, and create lifelong habits.

# 1

# THE SCIENCE BEHIND ADHD

" ADHD isn't a bad thing," said international pop star Adam Levine. To some of us, this may feel quite patronizing, leading us to wonder what a celebrity with so much money and fame would understand about ADHD.

Sometimes, it can be hard for us to imagine our favorite celebrities battling the same obstacles we have. Visualizing that person being a clutter bug or experiencing brain fog, when it feels like you're trying to complete a puzzle with missing pieces, can feel somewhat impossible. Nevertheless, this is not accurate.

Adam Levine is one of the many celebrities who has spoken openly about his journey with ADHD. In his early childhood, he realized he wasn't quite like the rest of his classmates. For instance, sitting down and concentrating on getting school-work done was an easy task for many, but it was an immense challenge for him. Fortunately, he had a support system and a doctor who provided him with coping mechanisms and treatment strategies. Adam continues his journey with ADHD even through adulthood. Just like many of us, his ADHD brain presents itself at work, in his case, sitting down and writing songs. Despite having a million and one ideas, putting pen to paper can feel grueling. Being open and honest about our cognitive challenges is undeniably a difficult task. It doesn't come easy for you or me, nor does it for someone with a huge platform like Adam Levine. Hence, the next time you feel alone in this journey, think of these words from Adam Levine: "Remember you are not alone. There are others going through the same thing."

## DEFINING ADHD

### A Neurodivergent Disorder

Neurodevelopmental disorders are conditions that affect the brain's ability to function. ADHD usually manifests from a young age, affecting 3–7% of children. The disorder can be categorized into four different subtypes: inattentive presentation, hyperactive presentation, combined presentation, and undefined presentation, all of which present symptoms such as irregular moods, difficulty concentrating, inability to follow directions, and staying still. The reason behind ADHD is still an ongoing debate amongst scientists and healthcare professionals; however, we do know that it is influenced by both genetic and environmental factors.

## Brain Region Development

According to Faraone, S. V., & Larsson, H. (2019), brains are significantly smaller in children diagnosed with ADHD, particularly in an area of the brain called the Frontostriatal network. The Frontostriatal network includes parts that are responsible for decision-making, regulating emotions, and how we move our body. In addition, Faraone, S. V., & Larsson, H. (2019) also found that the development of the outer layer of the brain, known as gray matter, developed roughly three years later in kids who were diagnosed with ADHD. This means that to compensate for slow growth, the brain attempts to use other parts that are not designed for those functions. In turn, this causes us to have difficulty concentrating and planning our bodily movements.

Furthermore, Silk, T. J., Vance, A., Rinehart, N., Bradshaw, J. L., & Cunnington, R. (2009) discovered that in a study involving 15 young males with ADHD, magnetic resonance imaging (MRI) found a considerable reduction in white matter. White matter is a crucial nerve fiber in the brain that allows both sides to communicate and exchange information efficiently. Specifically, the areas that are responsible for muscle movement and processing rewards. This means that insufficient communication between these areas is responsible for difficulties with planning, thinking, and managing our movements. For instance, imagine you enter a classroom or office in which you need to sit down and remain quiet. While one side of your brain has processed this information, it will take significantly longer for it to be communicated to the side that informs all of our muscles. This can explain why individuals with ADHD often take a little bit longer to process certain information and execute particular movements.

### Genetic Influence

Faraone, S. V., & Larsson, H. (2019) concluded that ADHD has a heritability rate of 74%, subsequently making it one of the highest genetically influenced disorders, though this cannot be attributed to one single gene. ADHD is frequently seen in multiple family members; you've probably noticed a pattern within your own family. Maybe your mum or uncle have similar ADHD tendencies as you? In an additional study, Faraone, S. V., & Larsson, H. (2019) found that certain genes are consistent with ADHD and symptoms such as substance abuse issues or antisocial behavior. Perhaps you can recall a family member who's always had trouble forming or maintaining friendships or relationships. By looking at our genetics, it becomes easier to assess and understand our ADHD symptoms, as well as what treatments will work best for us.

## COGNITIVE DIFFERENCES

### Executive Functioning

Executive functioning is a set of mental abilities that involve working memory, cognitive flexibility, and self-control. Essentially, it allows us to possess all the tools we need to be efficient at setting goals, planning, and getting things done. However, some people have executive dysfunction, where they struggle with important functions like memory, self-control, and cognitive flexibility. This can significantly impair an individual's daily life as it creates difficulty when deciding what to focus on or understanding that you need to complete certain tasks even when you don't want to. Think of it as a cognitive maze; for those with executive functioning, there is a clear and simple path out of the maze, but for those with executive dysfunction, the only path available is one that crosses a million other paths, making life confusing and challenging.

Executive dysfunction often paralyzes our ability to plan for activities that we need to complete. This means it can cause us to be significantly disorganized due to not allocating sufficient time to complete tasks or even attempting to complete multiple tasks at once. Healthcare providers often suggest leaving visual reminders in workspaces and at home. For example, sticky notes, to-do lists, or by setting daily reminders on your phone. Furthermore, things like clocks and alarms can be used as an external reminder of time.

### Working Memory and Inhibition

When executive dysfunction coincides with ADHD, it can often create a further battle with things like inhibition, working memory, organizing, and planning. For this reason, it's important to understand and analyze how it affects our cognitive process.

Our working memory allows us to remember and complete tasks simultaneously; for instance, when you read, you can remember the previous word because of your working memory. Those of us who have ADHD and executive dysfunction will often forget the tiniest detail and, in some cases, the most important detail. Additionally, sustaining attention on one singular task can feel extremely difficult. Our focus will usually shift from one activity to another without us even realizing it. This can also explain the lack of control we have over our inhibition. Our thoughts and emotions can run free in our minds. Meanwhile, our actions may be doing the same externally, making it an extreme challenge to resist impulses.

## EMOTIONAL CHALLENGES

### Emotional Dysregulation

If you have ever struggled to manage your own emotions, then it was probably due to emotional dysregulation. Every day, we engage in experiences, both internal and external, that trigger an emotional response. An external situation is something that exists outside of our immediate control, for instance, seeing your friend's organized house, subsequently leading you to feel upset about your untidy house. Internal situations are in our immediate control and influence, for example, positive thoughts about how well you are doing on your journey to an organized home.

There are multiple factors that influence how intense our emotions are and how well we can manage them. For example, a poor diet and a lack of sleep can heighten the intensity of our emotions, turning feelings of sadness into feelings of devastation. Alternatively, a good night's sleep and nutritious food incorporated into your diet will increase the number of positive hormones in your body and aid in self-regulation.

To put it simply, emotional dysregulation creates intense emotions. This, paired with our ADHD, can trigger an impulsive reaction. This combination can present itself as bouncing off the walls with joy or crying our eyes out. Thus, it creates a display of emotions that is unfitting for the situation. It is one of the most prevalent and demanding symptoms of ADHD.

It's vital that we understand the four key components of emotional dysregulation so we are not alarmed by our intense emotions when it comes to tackling obstacles related to cleaning and organizing. The four components consist of:

- **Inability to refocus attention:** For some of us, this may happen when we begin our journey with cleaning and organizing, as it is often accompanied by feeling overwhelmed and frustrated.
- **Emotional impulsiveness:** Inappropriate behavior when experiencing negative emotions. For instance, spontaneous outbursts, making rash decisions, or being reactive.
- **Inability to exchange negative emotions for more positive ones:** Personally, I struggled with this throughout high school, with one bad grade slowly turning into a continuous cycle of bad grades due to a belief that I was incapable of excelling. It was cemented into my brain that I was dumb and stupid, and it didn't

matter how many times a teacher told me I was smart or capable.

- **Inability to calm down after an emotionally provoking experience:** For instance, imagine that arguing with your friend has left you both feeling upset. While your friend could reason with the argument and calm down, you needed days or weeks to process and come to terms with it.

### *Label Your Emotions*

Gaining control and reinstating your power from emotional dysregulation is entirely achievable. One of the best ways to execute this is by labeling our emotions. This may sound silly, and you might even be thinking every adult knows how to say they feel tired or have a headache. However, delving deeper to understand the root emotion behind a response may shed light on why we react the way we do. For instance, I often struggle with feeling overwhelmed, usually causing headaches and a tight chest, but once I slow down and take a minute to process how I'm feeling, I can begin to understand the cause. Then, I can trace back these symptoms to anxiety and stress, subsequently creating a barrier between the emotion and my response. The process involves three simple steps: slowing down, tracing back to the "why?" and then labeling it with an emotion. Once we label what emotion led to our reaction, we can find a healthier way to deal with it. Creating the barrier between the emotion and the response will help us recognize the emotion when it comes and allow us to step back and choose a response different from the usual.

## PSYCHOLOGICAL INTERVENTIONS

### Cognitive Behavioral Therapy

Cognitive behavioral therapy is one of the most scientifically researched nonmedical treatments for ADHD. Researchers have discovered in studies with children that behavior modification can have a positive impact on relationships with their peers, teachers, and parents, as well as providing the individual with the necessary tools to overcome symptoms that are considered debilitating. Cognitive behavioral therapy involves the child and their support system learning techniques from a therapist to integrate into their day-to-day lives. It is based on goals that are set for an extended duration and slowly accomplished. The ultimate outcome is not only the child learning new behavior but also transforming their thoughts and attitudes. While this study focuses on children, it's also highly recommended for adults as it's a goal-oriented therapy that aims to convert negative thoughts into positive ones.

### Mindfulness and Self-Control

Self-regulation is the ability to manage our display of emotions in accordance with the situation that triggered those emotions. For many of us, that is a tricky task, but a great way to overcome this obstacle is by exploring mindfulness. Mindfulness focuses on taking our attention away from something emotionally stimulating and anchoring our mind to something else happening in the present moment, for instance, our breathing or what we can feel around us. It emphasizes the importance of considering our impulses before we act them out, as well as converting self-damaging thoughts into positive ones.

Furthermore, it is crucial that we enhance our executive functioning skills as this will become a valuable tool on our journey of organization and cleaning. Many of us who suffer from a lack of inhibitory control find it difficult to resist impulses. However, a simple yet silly game could help you improve your self-control. It involves a friend or family member, and both of you take turns telling jokes, but neither of you can laugh or smile. Think about it: You're resisting an impulse while training your brain at the same time. In addition, for those of us who want to improve our attention skills but can't find a partner to practice these games with, grab a bell and walk around attempting not to make a sound. This game will have you laser-focused!

## DEBUNKING ADHD MYTHS

### *Different Doesn't Mean Dumb*

An important part of understanding ADHD is also debunking the misconceptions surrounding it. ADHD is a medically recognized disorder; however, this doesn't mean that our peers comprehend the complexities of ADHD in the same way as medical professionals. This means that ADHD is often disregarded by our friends and family and not seen as a legitimate mentally impairing illness. In turn, we may find ourselves unfairly labeled as lazy or even stupid. While neurodivergent brains communicate and grow differently from neurotypical brains, there is no correlation with IQ, ensuring that these statements are profoundly inaccurate.

Have you ever been told to "try a little harder" or "just focus a bit more"? As a child, I'm sure you were misguided by these patronizing statements. Then, you were most likely contradicted by misconceptions about your hyperactivity. Personally, I grew up being stereotyped as that kid who couldn't stop moving during class. Maybe you have even been told you will outgrow it or heard that it only ever happens to boys. While we cannot control the thoughts of others and the harsh things they say, we can educate ourselves on the reality of our disorder. It is not something we will outgrow, nor is it something that only affects one gender. When incorporating the correct techniques and embracing our unique differences, ADHD becomes a source of empowerment and a true asset to our lives.

### Promote Awareness

Battling stigma is undeniably a difficult experience. It can often feel as if we're swimming against currents of bias and stereotypes, and then we are suddenly hit with a salty taste of criticism. Eventually, we reach the shore, where there's clarity and other neurodivergent swimmers who are just like us, people who can relate to and understand the complexities and symptoms of ADHD. As individuals who experience ADHD, it is our responsibility to spread awareness. One way we can break down these walls of stigma is by sharing our stories. While this can feel daunting, people want to hear your voice! However, for this to be effective, we must also educate ourselves so that when it comes to battling those pesky discriminators, we are fully equipped with knowledge and factual information.

### Real-Life With ADHD

The real-life experience of ADHD is one that will vary from person to person. However, I can guarantee that we have all experienced the agonizing challenge of staying organized. I am sure that, just like me, you have felt how hard it is to stay focused on one thing, internally beating yourself up for not being able to concentrate like your friends. Maybe you can even relate to the exhausting feeling of a constant racing mind, all while trying to remember coping strategies and ways to process emotions accurately. The daily life of a neurodivergent individual is one that can feel overwhelming and draining, but with a loving support system and an abundance of self-care, it is a unique path that we must embrace.

As we reflect on the complexities and nuances of ADHD, we can now harness our newly discovered knowledge to pave a path of self-love, compassion, and clarity. This enhanced understanding will allow us to not only excel on our journey to an improved life but also confidently leave the chaos behind us without fear or judgment. In the next chapter, we will be delving into strategies to help neuro-divergent individuals overcome common challenges as we learn to implement life-long habits. Remember, you are not the only one taming their river of fast-flowing thoughts and impulses, creating a path to the ultimate way of living.

2

# ADHD-TAILORED STRATEGIES

At one point in our lives, we have all felt like we were climbing a mountain, whether it was working toward a degree, recovering from a breakup, or even facing an illness. There are instances in which we all have faced an uphill battle. However, 21-year-old Danielle Fisher truly accomplished ascending to the world's largest mountain, Mount Everest. Like many of us, Danielle received her Attention Deficit Disorder (ADD) diagnosis in elementary school, navigating the challenges of medication that didn't suit her while scaling some of the world's highest peaks. Nevertheless, she confronted ADD the same way she would a mountain by tapping into her inner strength and immense determination, alongside having therapists and a loving support system. "I always tell my daughter not to give up. It's hard, but if you focus on one step at a time, you'll reach those mini-goals on the way up. Eventually, you'll get where you're going." I challenge you to use Danielle's story and her mother's words as inspiration. Though you may not be climbing Mount Everest, you are conquering an uphill journey. Let's leave the chaos at the foothills and rise above adversity to uncover an improved way of life.

## WHY IS CLEANING SO DIFFICULT?

Cleaning is the dreaded responsibility that I'm sure all of us would like to avoid. The new me would say cleaning is therapeutic and life-changing, but the old me would tell you it's tedious, boring, and overwhelming. After some time, I realized that these negative feelings were not universal, leading me to ask myself why I felt this way. Subsequently, I realized it wasn't me who hated cleaning; it was my ADHD brain. One of my biggest problems was focusing on the task at hand. I'd begin by washing dishes, go do laundry mid-way, and ultimately end up picking out weeds from my garden. On other days, I'd have a sudden urge to combat my bathroom, living room, and kitchen all at once, to then feel burnt out and like I hadn't really accomplished much. I was surrounded by so much clutter and mess that I didn't even know where to start. Evidently, I'd throw myself into cleaning without an end goal in sight. This vicious cycle of hyper-focusing one week to not focusing at all another week, mixed with a million and one negative feelings, grew exhausting. However, deep down, I knew that with the right strategies, our unique minds could overcome any struggle, including converting chaos into calm.

## ESTABLISH A ROUTINE

If you are anything like me, then you have experienced the endless loop of attempting to clean but never really accomplishing anything. This means that you also understand how important it is to implement strategies and boundaries when it comes to cleaning.

One of the most crucial tactics for cleaning is establishing a structured routine and maintaining consistency. This means creating a plan and dedicating certain days to certain chores. For example, I know I must wipe down my kitchen countertops everyday, but I will dedicate Tuesdays from 5:00 p.m. to 5:30 p.m. to vacuuming the kitchen and living room. Breaking down the task into smaller chunks and allocating time allows that daunting feeling to subside. Below is an example of assigning common chores a specific day of the week. A great way to ensure consistency is by having visual aids. This could be a planner or checklist that's on your wall, as well as daily scheduled reminders on your phone to alert you when it's time to begin.

## WEEKLY MAINTENANCE CHORES

| MONDAY | TUESDAY | WEDNESDAY | THURSDAY | FRIDAY | SATURDAY | SUNDAY |
|---|---|---|---|---|---|---|
| **OFFICE:**<br>• Declutter desk<br>• Sort emails<br>• Save any important files | **BATHROOM:**<br>• Disinfect toilet<br>• Clean shower and tub<br>• Wipe down mirror, counter, and sink | **BEDROOM:**<br>• Dust and vacuum<br>• Change bedding<br>• Tidy-up closets and drawers | **KITCHEN:**<br>• Clean out fridge<br>• Do any dishes<br>• Wipe counters and appliances | **FLOORS:**<br>• Clear any clutter<br>• Shake rugs<br>• Vacuum and sweep<br>• Mop | **LAUNDRY:**<br>• Collect all dirty laundry<br>• Sort into wash categories<br>• Wash<br>• Dry<br>• Put away | **DUST AND DECLUTTER:**<br>• Dust shelves, electronics, sills, fans, lights, etc.<br>• Tidy-up common spaces |
| Time of Day:<br>____:____ | Time of Day:<br>____:____ | Time of Day:<br>____:____ | Time of Day:<br>____:____ | Time of Day:<br>____:____ | Time of Day:<br>____:____ | Time of Day:<br>____:____ |

Another step to success with cleaning is prioritizing self-care, meaning it is time for you to start investing in your well-being. Practicing activities like exercising, meditation, and mindfulness are amazing for your brain. They have all been scientifically proven to decrease stress and aid with emotional regulation. In addition, invite your family and friends along with you on this journey to celebrate and support your small achievements. Recognizing your accomplishments will not only boost motivation but also foster a positive mindset. Remember, the best investment you can make is an investment in yourself.

## CHANNEL YOUR ENERGY

### *Hyperactivity and Impulsivity*

Hyperactivity can make tackling jobs like cleaning and organizing particularly hard. Have you ever noticed that relentless feeling like you just can't sit still? Maybe you've been in a store before and just couldn't resist the urge to touch everything within reach. You may have even been told you don't have a filter when it comes to blurting out answers or accidentally saying the wrong thing. That is hyperactivity, a very common symptom of ADHD, that can leave us feeling eager and restless. Hyperactivity usually stirs up a feeling of impulsivity, especially when we have big tasks in front of us, like decluttering our house. Subsequently, we will jump straight into the mess without a plan of action, and then, because we are so stressed and don't strategize, we begin jumping from one task to another. Ultimately, we become frustrated, overwhelmed, and inconsistent with any future cleaning.

Hyperactivity and impulsivity usually go hand in hand. Surprisingly, they can significantly influence our home and the mess inside of it. Impulsivity is where we tend to turn off our ears, get bored easily, lose anything and everything, as well as have poor attention to detail. You may have noticed this the last time you looked at your doom pile and wondered why there was a candle, a mismatched pair of socks, and your last utility bill all in one spot, along with a million other random items from your house unified into one pile. When we feel impulsive, we tend to contradict schedules and planning, and we envision ourselves as superheroes who can tackle every single cleaning task possible within a couple of hours.

### Harness Your Hyper-Focus

While there isn't a cure for ADHD symptoms, there are coping techniques that can make a positive impact on our everyday lives. One of the first strategies is implemented by minimizing distractions. This means that when the allocated time for vacuuming or decluttering begins, it's a great idea to put your phone on charge and out of reach or even turn the volume down on the TV or radio. This will allow you to focus on one task at a time.

Additionally, we can incorporate timers and alarms into our daily tasks. Inevitably, there is a never-ending list of cleaning tasks that we can do, making it essential that we manage our time correctly. One of my favorite ways to do this is by setting a timer. For example, unloading the dishwasher takes roughly four minutes. By setting an alarm, I'm making it a fun challenge for myself and having a constant reminder to beat the clock. Using an alarm allows us to maintain our hyper-focus by breaking down tasks into manageable and structured times. This is one of the best ways for us to channel our ADHD energy productively!

Furthermore, cognitive behavioral therapy, as mentioned in Chapter 1, involves empowering conversations with a therapist that will enhance mindful decision-making and separate undesirable behaviors from desirable ones. Moreover, regularly exercising is paramount for those of us with an ADHD brain, as well as eating healthy foods and ensuring you're getting enough sleep. These three activities alone will improve executive functioning. Sometimes, the most basic elements of our lives are the ones we need to improve. Don't overlook the wisdom in health is wealth.

## OVERCOME MEMORY CHALLENGES

### *Working Memory Deficits*

Working memory is what we use to hold small amounts of information while we are using it, for instance, remembering directions while you're driving. As we know from Chapter 1, many of us with ADHD brains experience the daily struggle of forgetting the tiniest detail due to our limited ability to retain it. This can significantly affect us when we attempt the simplest of tasks. For instance, when we try to clean our house and get distracted by a text or a knock on the door, leading to another distraction like making a drink or playing with the dogs. It becomes a repetitive cycle for a multitude of tasks we attempt in our day. Our short-term memory struggles to keep focus, and we end up forgetting the next item on the agenda, ultimately losing sight of the original goal. Personally, this makes me feel even more discouraged and stressed when I contemplate my next attempt.

### *Strengthen Your Memory*

If you believe that all hope for having an immensely strong and beyond-capable short-term memory has vanished, then you are mistaken. There are countless solutions to improving this, beginning with online games. Interactive games like chess, pattern recognition, and crossword puzzles allow your brain to find solutions for unique situations, in turn strengthening your memory. In addition, participating in regular exercise allows the brain to retrieve all necessary nutrients and blood flow to function at full capacity. Alongside cognitive behavioral therapy, where you'll revolutionize your thoughts and behavior, inevitably, you'll have a remarkable memory within no time.

### *Utilize Visual Cues*

As we work toward acquiring cognitive resilience, we can implement organizational techniques to help us. Firstly, using a handy notepad, diary, or even the notes section of your phone to write down important information when you receive it will allow you to stay aligned. Secondly, we must keep in mind that we do not need to multitask. This means tackling each task a step at a time. We can organize by urgency and dedicate time to each task, approaching them with a strategy and allowing for clarity. I've compiled a list of visual cues to make it a bit more straightforward:

- **Whiteboards:** A creative and fun way to place daily or weekly reminders.
- **Post-it notes:** Perfect for short reminders in the office. Remember not to get too post-it-note crazy, or you'll feel overwhelmed!
- **Digital reminders:** Apps such as Todoist are essential for daily reminders.
- **Labels:** Labels allow for clarity in boxes, baskets, bins, and even shelves.

## ATTENTION DIFFICULTIES

Have you ever been told that if you just turned off the TV or your phone notifications, you wouldn't be so easily distracted? While it is true that our surroundings contribute to our distractibility, those of us with ADHD will know that our brain chemistry won't always allow for undivided focus. As neurodivergent individuals, we are prone to being distracted, and it's significantly harder for us to get back on track once we've lost focus. Trust me; you're not the only one who found themselves cleaning the shower when they were supposed to be taking out the trash. Compared to neurotypicals, our ADHD brains have lower levels of the chemicals responsible for providing us the push to stay focused. This is why staying on task is especially difficult for us. Luckily, there are strategies to help us overcome these challenges.

### *Optimize Focus*

One of the contributing factors to distraction is jumping all in without prioritizing the main tasks. A great technique to combat this is using the Ivy Lee method. At the end of each day, write down your top six priorities, ranking them on urgency. The following day, you can complete the tasks at your own pace, and any that you weren't able to complete will move on to the following day's list.

We all experience times when emotions like anxiety, frustration, or sadness hold us back from tackling tasks that feel too large or overwhelming. However, there are strategies that can help motivate us through these stalled moments, even for jobs we may not enjoy, like cleaning. One way to conquer your emotional procrastination with cleaning is by writing down all those overwhelming feelings, which will allow you to process and acknowledge them in a safe and private way. Furthermore, you can use the Pomodoro technique of working for twenty-five minutes and resting for five minutes to break down your priorities into manageable time slots. Sticking to a timer like the Pomodoro method can help you avoid burnout by enforcing breaks at regular intervals.

### *Eliminate Distractions*

The key to enhanced focus is our environment. This implies that we must eliminate our distractions, even the simple ones such as the TV in the background, our email notifications dinging on our laptops, or even putting our pets in their beds for thirty minutes. Essentially, you need to reduce any disturbance that might distract you from reaching your ultimate goal of an organized life. In addition, having visual progress charts can not only help you stay mindful of your core objective but also understand what techniques do and don't work for you. During this journey, it's important we have self-compassion to avoid getting frustrated or upset if a certain strategy doesn't yield results for us like it has for someone else.

## HABIT STACKING

I used to find that I always had the enthusiasm and excitement to start new behaviors or activities, but I lacked the ability to stay consistent and incorporate them into my daily routine. While our old routines may be comfortable, growth only comes from change. Thus, we need to establish a plan that will set us up for success on our journey of change. This plan revolves around creating new habits by utilizing the power of our existing habits. Adopting new habits can be an uphill battle due to our inability to focus. One way to win this battle is to integrate habit stacking. The idea of habit stacking is to have one positive action followed by another.

Let's break it down into manageable steps:

1. Identify an existing habit.
2. Choose a new habit to implement.
3. Stack the new habit directly after the existing habit.

It follows a simple formula: After I [existing habit], I will immediately [new habit].

Habit stacking is a super effective technique as it allows us to associate our pre-existing habits with new ones. In turn, you slowly create a strong mental association between the two habits. It enforces a simple routine and encourages consistency. Remember to trust the process. Start small and aim for consistency, even if you're tired, stressed, or just don't want to. Over time, your new habits will empower you to cultivate a healthy and organized life. The table below provides some simple examples of habit stacking. For help staying consistent, you could also track your progress on a chart in your diary or with an app. Tracking your progress provides valuable feedback and allows you to adjust your system, ensuring that you will succeed.

## EXAMPLES OF HABIT STACKING

| Existing Habit | New Habit | Habit Stack |
|----------------|-----------|-------------|
| Brushing your teeth | Wipe down the sink | After I brush my teeth, I will immediately wipe down the sink. |
| Getting dressed | Make the bed | After I get dressed, I will immediately make the bed. |
| Hanging up keys | Sort the mail | After I hang up my keys, I will sort through my mail. |
| Eating dinner | Do the dishes | After I finish my dinner, I will immediately do the dishes. |
| Feeding pets | Tidy-up the living room | After I feed my pets, I will immediately tidy-up the living room. |

## MOTIVATION AND REWARD

### *Not Interested*

Being surrounded by a mess is probably familiar to you. While neurotypical people usually feel the need and desire to clean this mess, a neurodivergent person, such as yourself, will sit and wonder when you'll muster up the motivation. For some of us, that motivated feeling never comes, and we are once again left asking why. Perhaps this is because you're just not interested in the task at hand. One of ADHD's many symptoms is an interest-based nervous system. This means that only something you're really interested in or something that will provide immediate stimulation will trigger motivation. Thus, when you need to complete a seemingly mundane activity like organizing or cleaning, you're left feeling unmotivated.

### Find Motivation

As we embark on a journey of personal growth, we need to find ways we can trigger motivation so we can increase productivity as well as enjoyment. To cultivate intrinsic motivation, we must find ways to obtain personal satisfaction from organizing. My favorite way to do this is by taking before and after pictures. I begin by taking the before picture, setting my goal, and slowly progressing until I'm ready to take the after picture. Ultimately, I feel satisfied that I completed the task, and I have a visual reminder to see how much I accomplished and progressed. We also need to stimulate extrinsic motivation, which means feeling encouraged by external rewards. For instance, inviting your friends over once a month will motivate you to maintain a tidy house, and you will not only impress your friends by achieving such a huge goal, but you will also have a fun time.

### Treat Yo' Self

Persistence drives achievements; thus, it is vital we learn to stay consistent. This can be executed by reinforcing positive behavior using time-based rewards. For example, give yourself a five-minute break every twenty-five minutes. We can also implement progressive rewards every time we reach an organizational milestone. These rewards could be as small as getting a box of chocolates or as big as spending a day at an amusement park. Choose rewards that motivate you to reach the milestone and reinforce your healthy behaviors.

Now that we have a clear understanding of the strategies specifically for those with ADHD, we are well-equipped to unleash our full potential. By applying these strategies and techniques, we can harness elevated productivity as well as unparalleled excellence. In the next chapter, we will begin ascending the mountain and uncovering the ultimate wisdom behind eliminating clutter and sustaining hyper-focus. Let's kick things off in the heart of the house, the kitchen.

# 3

# KITCHEN

With twenty-three gold medals, global recognition, and the power to redefine competitive sports, Michael Phelps is an extraordinary man who is globally recognized for exceptional swimming and natural talent. Would you believe me if I told you that the same man was bullied at school for an inability to sit still and stay focused? The same man, who is now known for being the most brilliant Olympian of all time, was told he would never be able to focus on anything because of ADHD. Thankfully, the diagnosis inspired him and his mother, motivating them to prove everyone wrong. Take a plunge like Michael Phelps, defy the odds, and shatter the low expectations.

## ASSESS AND PLAN

### *Identify Pain Points*

The first stop on our journey of cleanliness and organization is the kitchen, the heart of our house, where we often spend a lot of time nourishing our bodies and minds with rich foods. Creating a healthy lifestyle and implementing new habits like exercising and improving productivity becomes nearly impossible if we have dangerous bacteria climbing all over our food each time we cook. Germs will not only make us sick for a couple of days, but they can also lead to life-threatening illnesses.

To counteract these pesky bacteria, we need to consider three different categories within our kitchen: functionality, cleanliness, and safety. Functionality means considering if everything in your kitchen works. Over time, we often have the tendency to accumulate things we don't need, or that don't work. Cleanliness really is as simple as it sounds. Consider removing the clutter you have on your countertops. Safety involves making our kitchen accessories easily accessible yet appropriately stored.

Let's assess our kitchen pain points by asking ourselves the following questions:

- Is the sink always full of dirty dishes?
- Are there always crumbs on the countertops and floor?

- Are there piles of homeless items scattered around your counters?
- Do you have grease or dust collecting on your countertop appliances?
- Are utensils, pots, and pans, as well as spices and cooking oils, within reach?
- Are you collecting too many mixing bowls, mugs, or plates?
- Is the trash can constantly overflowing?

### Set Realistic Goals

Our central focus for our first area of cleaning and organizing is maintaining clarity and focus, ultimately building up motivation to yield success. To achieve this, we need to set attainable goals. This means that while you have the heart to shoot for the stars and conquer every task, you need to be realistic about what you can manage. Especially considering a lot of us have jobs, kids, pets, and further responsibilities. Setting lofty and unrealistic goals from the start can lead to burnout and disappointment. It is better to set and succeed at a small goal that will drive you to go bigger the next time than to set an unattainable goal and feel like a failure. Allow yourself to feel accomplished and successful by starting small.

## DECLUTTER

### *Plan for Function*

Typically, we can spend up to several hours a day in our kitchens; hence, creating a clean and clutter-free zone is the ideal solution. To execute this successfully, we need a strategic plan, starting with setting our kitchen goals. What do you want to achieve in your kitchen? Some of us might want a time-efficient space so we're not spending hours making packed lunches or cooking dinners. The rest of us might want a creative oasis where we can become better cooks and bake as many sweet treats as our heart desires. Once we've accomplished clarity through setting goals, we will begin clearing the chaos and clutter.

### *Minimize and Categorize*

Evolving from chaos to structure means clearing your kitchen of all the items that do not belong there: keys, utility bills, screwdrivers, batteries, and anything else that you wouldn't use to make food. We also need to comprehend the spatial limits of our kitchen; we must understand that our cabinets and drawers can only fit so many pots and pans before they become overwhelming and messy. Furthermore, we will need to designate a place for each item. Consider where you would like cups and plates, as well as your pots and pans. Remember, these locations should be based on efficiency; your frying pans should not be far away from the stove. Part of the kitchen clean-up is also clearing out any expired food you've accumulated. The best way to tackle this is by pulling out every food item and checking the expiry date. Plastic bins are super useful at categorizing each food group, as well as labeling the expiry date, so you'll be less likely to let the food go to waste.

When we look at our utensils, gadgets, and cookware, we must reflect on our kitchen goals and ask ourselves if we really need them. While I love having the option of five different mixing bowls, I only need my two favorite ones. Another important aspect is minimizing visual distractions; menus stuck to your fridge and pizza magnets holding up your kid's artwork can contribute to a stressful and unorganized environment. Allow yourself to say goodbye to those items you feel obliged to keep. Do you really need a teapot when you don't even like tea? You can also use tape to analyze what you use throughout the year. Place a strip of tape on each item, remove it when you use it, and a year later, you'll be able to see what you haven't touched.

## SIMPLIFY STORAGE

### Storage Solutions

Have you ever related to the idiom out of sight, out of mind? Forgetting that an item exists just because you can't see it. Well, I have, but now I combat that pesky habit of mine with a baker rack. A baker rack is the optimal solution to open storage, allowing our cooking essentials to be visible and within reach. In addition, using hooks nearby for oven mitts can create a safer environment by triggering your memory before you reach into the oven to grab that hot tray. For myself, I've found that simply by having my oven mitts draped over the oven door handle, I'm always reminded to put them on before opening the oven. Simplicity is key when creating spaces for easy access. Thus, labeling where everything goes is a must. Transparent containers are perfect for organizing your fridge or pantry. You will be able to see exactly what's inside each container instead of experiencing the daily struggle of digging through your fridge or scanning your pantry.

### Establish Zones

As part of your organized system, it can be beneficial to create zones within your kitchen where particular items are stored and used for easy access and to avoid any accidents. Your cooking zone should be near the stove, and this is where you store all your pots, pans, oven mitts, utensils, and spices. If you enjoy baking, you will benefit from a separate baking zone near your mixer. You can store your baking utensils, bowls, and ingredients nearby. For prepping food, you can assign a zone where you keep all your cutting boards, knives, Tupperware, silverware, plates, and glasses. Even your sink area can be utilized as a zone for cleaning and doing the dishes. Here, you can store all cleaning products safely away from food preparation areas and close by for easy access.

## ESTABLISH ROUTINES

Our ADHD brains often make it difficult for us to follow through with tasks, so why not create a routine that facilitates task execution? The routine consists of four main points. The first part of this routine will require discipline and commitment, so grab your checklist and start achieving your new nightly goals. You will begin by loading the dishwasher and allowing all your dirty dishes to be cleaned overnight. Then, you will have clear countertops to disinfect and wipe down. However, we usually accumulate a lot of crumbs and dirt throughout the day, so grab your broom and give your kitchen a sweep. Lastly, take out the trash. This simple fifteen-minute routine keeps your kitchen a clean slate for the next time you use this space.

Fifteen-minute kitchen routine:

1. Load the dishwasher
2. Wipe counters
3. Sweep the floor
4. Take out the trash

While we all can acknowledge and appreciate the value of a structured cleaning routine, it's just as important that we cultivate healthy habits in our kitchen. For instance, cleaning utensils and pots and pans as we cook. Simply wash the items you're done using while your meal is cooking. This one small habit will take your sink from being consistently dirty and full to always empty and clean. If we have all of our kitchen tools nice and clean, it makes completing our routine even easier, as there won't be piles of pots and pans waiting to be washed.

## Break Down Tasks

It's easy to feel overwhelmed when looking at all the organizational and decluttering tasks that need to be done. But trying to tackle everything at once is a recipe for burnout and guilt. Instead, focus on taking small, consistent actions. Break big goals like decluttering the whole house down into bite-sized pieces. For example, commit to spending just 10 minutes per day decluttering—maybe focus on one drawer or shelf at a time. Or schedule a quick 5-minute tidying session in the evening to pick up clutter. Little actions add up over time. Be patient with yourself and celebrate small wins, like finally organizing that junk drawer or donating a bag of old clothes. Approaching chores this way prevents the mess from becoming unmanageable again. And you get the satisfaction of gradually making progress. So don't be intimidated by the big picture—take pride in those small decluttering accomplishments.

## Maintenance Habits

Naturally, there are areas of our kitchen that won't require a daily cleaning. For instance, a microwave can be cleaned once a week with water and lemon juice at a high temperature for three minutes, proceeding with a wipe down. In addition, a fridge only requires a deep clean every 2–3 months. However, you must ensure you've carefully labeled and organized your food to steer clear of mold and wasted food. Complete a weekly scan for expired or stinky foods in your fridge and throw them out, particularly before trash collection day.

So long as we stay on track with routines that practice small yet effective habits, a weekly clean will no longer require excessive amounts of time or energy.

## CREATE A REMINDER SYSTEM

Now, we know that incorporating a fifteen-minute routine into our night will allow for maximum clarity and productivity the following day. Let's get our agendas or planners and schedule our evening routines. Additionally, this book provides specific checklists at the end of each room chapter to help you clean and organize throughout your home.

Inevitably, there is a never-ending list of cleaning tasks that we can do, making it essential that we manage our time correctly. One of my favorite ways to do this is by setting a timer. For example, unloading the dishwasher takes roughly four minutes; by setting an alarm, I'm making it a fun challenge for myself and having a constant reminder to beat the clock.

Embrace the power of transformation as you convert your kitchen from chaos to calm. Implementing our new lifestyle means you have created a revolutionized space in your house, allowing you to create food that will nurture your body and soul. Through the simplicity of decluttering and organizing, as well as maintaining a cleaning routine, you have reclaimed time and uncovered a newfound happiness. Reward yourself for this tremendous effort. I'm sure a lot of us have validated capabilities that our loved ones didn't know we had. As we say goodbye to the kitchen, prepare yourself to say hello to the bedroom.

# KITCHEN CHECKLIST

This checklist is NOT meant to be completed in one day. Success comes through small consistent actions and not through big burnout sessions.

**Helpful tips:**

- STAY IN THE KITCHEN: Do not leave to re-home something until the kitchen is complete.
- Listen to music, books, or podcasts to make it fun.
- Adopt the minimalist mindset: be serious about getting rid of things that no longer serve you.

Identify pain points:
_____
_____

Set Realistic Goals:
_____
_____

Plan how you will overcome distraction and stay on task:
_____
_____

- [ ] Collect and clean all the dishes .

- [ ] Get three boxes and label them *Re-home, Trash, and Donate*. This will keep you from leaving the room.

- [ ] Establish Zones: plan where you will store items based on their function and location.

- [ ] Clear counters: go through every single thing on your countertops and only keep what belongs in the kitchen.

- [ ] Cupboards: go through one at a time and eliminate what is never used.

- [ ] Drawers: go through one at a time and eliminate what is never used.

- [ ] Return everything to the cupboards and drawers and organize into the established zones.

- [ ] Fridge: take everything out, throw away all expired food, and wipe down the shelves and drawers. Return and organize food.

- [ ] Pantry: take everything out and throw away all expired food. Vacuum or wipe down shelves. Return and organize everything by its category.

- [ ] Plan a specific time each week to clean and tidy the kitchen so the organization is maintained: Day of week:_____ Time:_____

- [ ] Disperse the three boxes: throw away trash, drop-off donations, and re-home the items that did not belong in the kitchen.

# 4

# BEDROOM

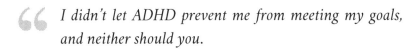 *I didn't let ADHD prevent me from meeting my goals, and neither should you.*

— HOWIE MANDEL

The wise words of a man who comes from an era where ADHD didn't even have a name. Through fear of being labeled crazy and receiving judgmental looks, Howie concealed his ADHD as much as he possibly could. While TV shows like Deal or No Deal allowed him to excel with movement and energy, scripted movies felt terrifying and required immense determination. His unavoidable ADHD symptoms left him blurting out on live television that he had OCD. Thankfully, his most common response was "Me too!" signifying that not one of us is truly alone in this journey.

## ASSESS YOUR BEDROOM

### *Identify Pain Points*

Stepping into your bedroom should feel like a warm space of tranquility and peace; it should not be an environment contaminated with doom piles and numerous projects we've started but never finished. Our ADHD tendencies shape the space and energy within a room, causing a place like our bedrooms to be disorganized and distracting, creating a poor sleeping environment. Thus, as we begin redefining this space, we must ask ourselves the following questions:

- What do I want from my bedroom?
- How big is my bedroom?
- Do I have space to reorganize furniture?
- Do I feel inspired and motivated by my current room? Is this the ideal room to begin and end each day?
- Are my clothes constantly piling up?
- Do I have enough storage or clothes hangers?
- Are my clothes organized by seasons or mixed together, creating chaos?

### *Set Realistic Goals*

Cultivating a bedroom that aligns with your emotional needs as well as goals and preferences can be a little tricky. In terms of atmosphere, we need to ask ourselves how the items within our bedroom make us feel. Do the family photos or posters make you feel happy or untidy? Are there too many colors causing you to feel overstimulated? We also need to consider functionality and think about where your bed and furniture are placed. Can you walk around without bumping into anything? Is your bed in an awkward place? Lighting should also be taken into consideration, as natural lighting is super important for our mental health.

Drastic overnight changes are unlikely to stick. Instead, aim for small, attainable targets and set yourself realistic goals. For example, a realistic goal would be to spend 10 minutes sorting and putting away the laundry pile each night. An unrealistic goal would be to completely declutter and organize the entire bedroom in one day. Build momentum with small victories and set a specific area of focus in your realistic goals.

## CLEAR THE CLUTTER

A systematic approach to decluttering our bedroom will provide us with goals and clarity. The first step to decluttering is removing snack wrappers and random knick-knacks from your nightstand and the tops of all your furniture. Next, we can relocate any items that don't belong in your bedroom, for example, exercise equipment, food, and dirty shoes, to a new home. We can also relocate any dirty laundry that might be on the floor or in the hamper to the washing machine. Now that our surroundings are clutter-free and clean, we can begin going through each piece of furniture, one drawer or shelf at a time. Ask yourself if the items inside belong in your bedroom; if they don't, set them aside to relocate after the current task is done.

Do not relocate each item you find right away! This will inevitably lead to distractions. Instead, create piles as you go through your furniture. Designate a pile for each category: Keep, relocate, donate, and throw away. I recommend using boxes or baskets to sort these piles so they are easy to transport.

### Minimize and Categorize

I can guarantee we can all think of clothes in our closet that we've never worn, yet we have somehow convinced ourselves there will be a special occasion to wear them on. While our brains could imagine a million and one reasons not to throw away these clothes that probably still have the labels on, are they worth the clutter and space in your wardrobe? Repurposing clothes can be even more beneficial than collecting dust. While old clothes can be donated, new clothes you never wear could be sold. If you love clothes, you most likely love accessories, too, but do you love the clutter that comes with them? I have lost countless numbers of bracelets and earrings just because I'd leave them scattered everywhere. The only way I could save my wallet and my time was by creating a designated tray or a cute bowl for my accessories.

We are constantly evolving and growing, so it only makes sense that our environment is as well. This means that sometimes we need to let go or organize and store items we don't necessarily need at this moment. For example, I know I do not need my winter clothes to consume my entire wardrobe in the middle of summer. Thus, I chose what I would like to keep for the following winter, packed them away into a box, labeled them, and put them somewhere safe and dry, such as my attic. This can also be applied to items like books, shoes, and blankets.

## STORAGE SOLUTIONS

After repurposing clothes and accessories we no longer need, we can still find ourselves burdened with heaps of closet items to organize. This means we need to take full advantage of every nook and cranny. Maximizing space means folding those sweaters and jeans that don't necessarily need to be hung up. We can also place shoes and handbags in storage containers with labels or designated colors. Furthermore, make sure to really evaluate your clothes hangers. While it may sound a bit silly, old, thick, or wooden hangers can take up a significant amount of space. We can also make use of our closet doors by using adhesive racks and hooks; this especially comes in handy for lint rollers or sewing kits.

### Seasonal Items

Establishing a designated place for seasonal items provides mental clarity and a clean atmosphere. An example of this is stashing away our off-season clothes under our bed. This does not mean chucking all the clothes in a trash bag, sliding it under your bed, and hoping for the best. It entails keeping an organized structure; if we store our winter clothes, we should separate winter shoes, jackets, and pants. We can then label the containers and slide them under our bed. When winter approaches, we will be able to easily transfer them back into our closet. We can integrate this routine into multiple areas of our bedrooms, so look out for empty drawers, trunks, and spaces that will aid in becoming clutter-free.

**Be Consistent**

Maintaining order involves consistency and discipline. Many of us feel like navigational systems, as our ADHD symptoms cause us to take a million and one detours. At the same time, neurotypical individuals can quickly get from point A to point B. While our faulty navigation will attempt to stay consistent, it won't always promise the fastest route. This can feel frustrating, but we should consider the journey this detour takes us on and the growth it allows us to build from. You may not follow through with new cleaning habits daily, but the critical part is getting back on track the following day. Those are the days that truly matter and will feel beyond rewarding.

## PROMOTE RELAXATION

**Bedding**

The mattress we sleep on and the material of our bed sheets can determine whether we have a day full of energy and positivity or a day that feels tiresome and grueling. For this reason, it's crucial we choose our bedding wisely. Bedding preferences are subjective and based on individual taste; some of us love fluffy pillows and soft blankets that feel like a warm embrace, while others prefer a hard pillow and refreshingly cool sheets. Cotton, linen, and bamboo sheets are optimal for breathability and softness, whereas flannel is a heavy fabric that will keep you warm and snug. For inexpensive sheets, try polyester; it is easy to wash, long-lasting and retains heat.

### Make Your Bed

We have all struggled with mess and being unorganized, but simplicity is key. This means we don't need ten different variations of pillows and blankets on our bed that will ultimately end up scattered across the floor. What we do need is a morning routine that involves making our bed. Making your bed is a small task that will provide a sense of accomplishment as well as a productive mindset. In addition, we often chuck things on our bed because it's easy and available space, but if we already have a tidy, respected bed, we will want to maintain it.

## DEVELOP DAILY HABITS

A morning and evening routine for cleaning your bedroom doesn't have to be as time-consuming as it sounds. After deep cleaning and disregarding all the clutter, maintaining a healthy living environment is the easiest part. Keeping your room tidy begins with making your bed every morning, a simple yet effective act of self-care. In the evening, once you've changed your work clothes or had a shower, make sure you either throw your clothes into a hamper or hang them back up. The remaining part of the routine consists of habits that we must learn to integrate daily. Putting away any clean laundry immediately is vital; it will prevent piles of washing from accumulating and creating an even bigger task.

*Your Room's Purpose*

Throughout our house, we need to make conscious choices to ensure that each room in our house serves its intended purpose effectively. For example:

- Kitchen and dining room: Cooking and food consumption
- Living room: Entertainment
- Bedroom: Sleep and relaxation
- Bathroom: Grooming and self-care
- Office: Work, projects, and schoolwork

The primary function of a bedroom is sleeping and relaxation. Engaging in activities like working, eating, or watching TV in this space can cause our brain to associate the room with these actions. As a result, we might struggle to sleep and relax in the very room where this is the intended purpose. By separating the functions and allocating rooms, we will further improve our mental health as well as limit clutter.

*Break Down Tasks*

By incorporating small cleaning tasks into your daily routines, you'll cultivate a bedroom that will become your sanctuary. We all know that a leading factor to a messy room is garbage; we often find receipts stored in the most random places and flyers piling up on our nightstands. The solution is putting a mini garbage can in your bedroom, one that will bear the burden of receipts and tissues instead of your floor. However, do not let it overflow; you must check it every day to ensure your bedroom stays clean and remove it as soon as it becomes full. Another habit involves making a list of daily chores for your bedroom, for example, taking out the bin, hanging up clothes, and taking the hamper to the washroom. You can even add a timer to ensure you accomplish these tasks and manage your time effectively.

### Maintenance Habits

Weekly habits will provide us with a structured framework, one that will prevent huge masses of mess and a build-up of chores that become overwhelming. In our bedrooms, we must change our bed sheets once a week. As we sleep, our body sheds dead skin cells as well as natural body oils and sweat. A build-up can cause dust mites, a smelly mattress, and even acne.

In addition, we need to vacuum and mop the floors to prevent dust, allergies, and bacteria from growing. By starting with decluttering and optimizing your layout, then integrating small, consistent cleaning tasks into your daily and weekly routines, you can create a bedroom sanctuary that supports your mental health and provides a relaxing, clutter-free space for rest and rejuvenation.

## MANAGE YOUR ENVIRONMENT

### *Set Digital Boundaries*

While we all love to sit in bed in comfy clothes, stick on our favorite Netflix series, and maybe even indulge in some chocolate, is it really the best idea?

Sleeping and watching TV in our beds can distort our melatonin production; this is the chemical that is released once we get into our comfy duvet and turn the lights off. It essentially regulates our circadian cycle and tells us it's time to sleep. However, if we are constantly overstimulated by TV and phone lights, it will greatly impact the quality of our sleep, leading to sleep deprivation. I would be lying if I said I never partake in watching my show in bed, although I have now placed boundaries. My boundaries consist of planning what I'm going to watch and limiting my exposure to it. For example, if I decide to watch my show in bed, I will set myself a limit of one episode that is thirty minutes long. In the following days, I'll make sure to limit my screen time in my bedroom and use my living room instead. This allows for a structured but relaxing environment.

TV is not the only device that can cause problems when it comes to sleeping. Another contributing distraction is our phones; receiving texts, emails, and notifications from apps can all cause a poor sleep cycle. Phones also bring with them the temptation to doom scroll social media when we should be sleeping. One way we can prevent this is by designating an area of our homes to charge our phones overnight. For instance, I like to place my phone in the kitchen, especially now that I have clear and clean countertops. If you're worried about not hearing your alarm from another room, consider investing in a simple alarm clock. You could even place the alarm clock across the room, far out of reach, so you are forced to get up and turn it off.

### *Promote Relaxation*

Implementing a nightly self-care routine will allow you to relax, unwind, and become liberated from the day's stress. As we know, lighting is crucial for our mental health; however, it can also affect how we sleep. When you're ready to unwind, make sure you dim the lights to create a relaxing atmosphere, and maybe even grab a nice cup of herbal tea to enhance relaxation. After this, it is important we don't contradict our previous actions with an over-stimulating phone, laptop, or TV. We must find calming activities that can be used as a substitute. One of my favorite things to do before bed is to practice mindfulness. This helps manage my ADHD symptoms and provides me with a mindset of gratitude as I wind down from the day. For nights that I would like to disconnect, I switch to reading a book.

## DEDICATE TIME

Our ADHD brain often causes us to forget the tiniest details; to maintain consistency with cleaning, we must plan out our weeks and months accordingly. To do this, you can either use an app, such as a digital reminder, or you can use a physical planner. Once we've determined our preferred method, we need to allocate specific days and weeks to different chores. For instance, I like to have Sunday resets, where I do multiple tasks around my house, including cleaning my bed sheets. This means every Sunday, I have allotted time in my calendar to clean my bed. In terms of the big decluttering, I believe a seasonal cleaning is best. Once the season changes, I open my diary and find a couple of days that I can dedicate to reorganizing and ensuring that I'm sticking to a clutter-free lifestyle. Decluttering every season helps us avoid the overwhelming and sporadic cleaning sessions that are responsible for our feelings of dread.

Just like Howie Mandel, you have excelled and achieved your goals. Not only have you created a chaos-free kitchen but also a calm bedroom. Now that you have incorporated these organizational strategies and methods, be prepared to experience a level of sleep quality that surpasses anything you have experienced before. Relish in the tranquility of your new sanctuary; you deserve it! In the next chapter, we will be deep cleaning the bacteria playground, also known as your bathroom.

# BEDROOM CHECKLIST

This checklist is NOT meant to be completed in one day. Success comes through small consistent actions and not through big burnout sessions.

**Helpful tips:**

* STAY IN THE BEDROOM: Do not leave to re-home something until the bedroom is complete.
* Listen to music, books, or podcasts to make it fun.
* Adopt the minimalist mindset: be serious about getting rid of things that no longer serve you.

Identify pain points:

_____
_____

Set Realistic Goals:

_____
_____

Plan how you will overcome distraction and stay on task:

_____
_____

☐ Make sure you have your three boxes labeled *Re-home, Trash, and Donate*. Have a laundry basket handy for clothing items.

☐ Floor: go through everything covering the floor and sort it into the boxes.

☐ Nightstand/desk: clear off and sort through any drawers. Wipe down the surfaces. Return and organize the items that belong in the bedroom.

☐ Dresser: clear off the surface, only keep what brings you joy. Go through drawers and donate any clothes that you haven't worn in a year.

☐ Closet: take out any items that do not belong in the bedroom. Sort through your clothes and donate any that you have not worn in a year. Return and organize items and clothing based on their category.

☐ Electronics: reduce clutter from wires by using wire boxes or ties. Reduce digital stimuli by removing any electronics that do not support a relaxing environment.

☐ Bedding: change/wash your bedding or get new bedding if needed.

☐ Decor: enhance or reduce the decor depending on your personal stimuli. Less is more.

☐ Plan a specific time each week to clean and tidy the bedroom and bedding so the organization is maintained: Day of week:_____ Time:_____

☐ Disperse the three boxes: throw away trash, drop-off donations, and re-home the items that did not belong in the bedroom. Put away any loose laundry from the basket.

# 5

# BATHROOM

 *I can only assume what normal is.*

— JEFFERY SIEGEL

Normal is the word that keeps us contained and locked up in a box. It's a word that is so simple yet so complex, aiming to set the requirements of who you should be. Conforming to societal standards, suppressing your unique qualities, and attempting to feed the hunger you have to fit in are all prerequisites. But who does this benefit? Uniqueness is powerful. Sharing compassion and love for individuality and others' thoughts, feelings, and interests are all what makes us human. Welcome your ADHD and admire the symptoms that set you apart from everyone else; uniqueness is inspiring.

## ASSESS YOUR BATHROOM

### *Identify Pain Points*

When evaluating our bathroom, we should ask ourselves the following questions:

- Who is using the bathroom?
- What kind of atmosphere do you want your bathroom to have? Energetic? Relaxing?
- Can everyone easily reach their bathroom necessities?
- Are my cabinets filled with expired medication and beauty products?
- Is my shower curtain growing mold?
- Do I have sufficient lighting to shave or apply makeup?

Consider where the daily struggles in your bathroom are; maybe your cabinet drawers are filled with expired junk, or you're fighting a constant battle with everyone leaving tissues and ear swabs everywhere. Locate the weaknesses so we can convert them into strengths.

### *Plan for Purpose*

Now, we must reflect on our answer to who is using the bathroom. If your answer involves children, we need to incorporate organizational methods for items like toothbrushes that are easy to use and accessible. Not only will this make your life simpler, but it also conveys an important message of priori-

CHAOS TO CALM | 65

tizing cleanliness. We can section off our bathroom into three different purposes: using the toilet, using the sink, and bathing. Analyze these three factors and determine what you want to be doing each day at each station. We already know the toilet only has one use, but an area like the sink can be quite diverse. Will you be using this area to put on your makeup, use the first aid kits, or groom your beard? Or will you simply be washing your hands? Apply the same method to our remaining section; the answers will be vital for understanding our storage needs.

### Areas of Focus

Ventilation, lighting, and accessibility are crucial points we must take into account. For those of us who love a hot and steamy bath or shower, ventilation is paramount for preventing moisture. A build-up of moisture in our bathrooms can lead to excessive amounts of mold and mildew. Leaving wet towels or floor mats in the wrong place or blocking our vent and window are the leading contributors. Proper lighting decreases the risk of accidents, especially when we are shaving, applying makeup, or just tired. It can also convey a multitude of moods; for instance, a dull white light might make your bathroom appear grimy and gray, while vibrant lighting creates an energizing, spa-like atmosphere.

Accessibility in the bathroom is about more than mobility features—it's about keeping necessities readily available. Make sure toilet paper, soaps, shampoos, and other shower essentials are stocked and stored in easy-to-reach areas. No more midnight searches under the sink when you run out of toilet paper. Keeping hygiene and beauty products organized in cabinets, shelves, and shower caddies prevents frustration. With your most used items accessible, you can spend less time hunting and more time enjoying your bathroom.

## CLEAR THE CLUTTER

Our bathrooms are usually filled with expired junk that is difficult to create an emotional attachment to, making this process even easier for us. However, before we jump in and start tossing out what we no longer need, we must refer back to our goals. Keep in mind what you want from this bathroom and how you are going to split tasks into manageable steps and include breaks.

We begin decluttering by opening up our cabinets and drawers, taking everything out, and checking the expiry date. Medicine past its expiry date is no longer effective, just like expired makeup or beauty supplies can give you a weird rash or an allergic reaction. Be sure to throw away any obvious trash, such as old toothbrushes, empty shampoo bottles, and used disposable razors. In addition, we can scan our bathroom for unnecessary clutter; maybe you have too many candles, fake plants, or trinkets on shelves.

### *Sort and Categorize*

Once we have defined what we are keeping, we can begin organizing. When organizing our bathroom cupboards and drawers, we need to keep certain categories grouped together. This means your makeup shouldn't be intertwined with a number of hair accessories and medications; they should all be separated into their assigned category. Inevitably, if we have large open spaces in our cabinets, things can become messy very quickly. For this reason, investing in a few acrylic containers or organizational bins will make converting chaos to calm much easier.

## STORAGE SOLUTIONS

Organizing our bathroom can be exciting; there are now multiple options available to place all our things, and we are so close to finishing. However, we need to take it step by step, follow the natural flow of the bathroom, and really consider where we want our belongings. Consider what tools we can use to not only implement order but maintain it. Do you ever find that your towels are just scattered everywhere in your linen closet? A tireless conflict between you and a piece of fabric. Well, the solution just might be a towel holder, which comes in all shapes and sizes and maintains a rolled towel perfectly. Towels aren't the only things that can look unsightly in the bathroom. Personally, I hate seeing my toilet cleaning products and toilet brush on show. So, I invested in a toilet paper stand, a slim cabinet that conceals my bathroom secrets, fitting right between the toilet and sink.

As we have learned, we must keep our bathroom belongings categorized in their own designated area. Nevertheless, some items are more challenging to organize, probably because we are either constantly using them or they simply do not fit in a storage container. For instance, bathrobes should be stored somewhere clean and high up to avoid being dragged on a dirty floor. Thus, hooks are the ideal solution. There is a wide variety of hooks, so don't worry if you're awful with power tools; a simple adhesive hook or one that hangs from the top of your door will work perfectly. Additionally, you can invest in adhesive shower trays, which are perfect for hanging your items above the water line and avoiding a rapid spread of mildew. For bath lovers, your everyday shower gel and loofah can be stored in a fashionable yet organized bath tray.

Constructing a framework for consistency involves making bathroom appliances easily accessible and neatly stored. It's a given that a house with a million and one storage containers on show isn't always the prettiest. For those of us who have open storage or cabinets without built-in storage, a sink fabric skirt could save your eyes. Sink fabric skirts are affordable cover-ups for undesirable parts of your sink by using cute patterns and fabrics. Tiered stands are also a graceful way to keep items like Q-tips, toilet rolls, or pretty soaps on display, all while maintaining an illusion of order.

## CREATE ROUTINES

### Set Reminders

Wiping down the mirror, disinfecting the sink, and scrubbing the toilet are tasks that are easy and simple for neurotypicals but extraneous and demanding for our ADHD brains. In previous chapters, we discovered how notepads and physical diaries are a great way to plan out a cleaning schedule.

However, we need to take full advantage of the built-in erasable whiteboard we have in our bathrooms: the mirror. A mirror is a fun and creative way to write notes and even things we need to do in our bathrooms. It also functions as a visual cue, so each time you enter the bathroom, your task is staring right back at you. Maybe even go to your local art store and grab some colorful whiteboard markers; with a swipe of your finger, they can easily be erased.

### Break Down Tasks

Fortunately, the bathroom is a small area, so it's not as taxing to clean as other rooms. My favorite way to clean my bathroom is by breaking it down into sections: sink and cabinets, toilet, and shower.

When cleaning our sink and cabinets, we begin by clearing the area and ensuring everything is organized. Then, it is crucial that we disinfect any nasty bacteria on the countertops and scrub the faucet handles and drain. The toilet usually remains clutter-free, meaning we should begin by cleaning the interior with a toilet bowl disinfectant and giving it a good scrub. Make sure to wash your hands, and then proceed with disinfecting the exterior. In addition, the shower requires a spray of disinfectant on the tub, tiles, faucet, and handles. Let it sit for a few minutes, and then begin scrubbing. Once you've finished, rinse the shower down with water.

## *Prevent Build-Up*

Cleaning the bathroom is usually a weekly task while clearing countertops and maintaining bathroom hygiene are things we should be considerate of every day. This will ensure you stay healthy and don't pass harmful bacteria from the bathroom into other rooms. Remember to utilize habit stacking here. The bathroom is the perfect place for this due to the many routines and habits that we already have in this room. Now, we just need to stack new little cleaning habits onto our existing ones: after I brush my teeth, I will wipe down the mirror. After I wash my hands, I will wipe down the sink and counter.

## PROMOTE DAILY ORDER

### *Maintenance Habits*

The bathroom is a high-traffic area, which allows us to feel and look our best. Nonetheless, the countless number of objects we pick up and use can cause a tremendous amount of clutter. For instance, imagine you shave your beard or legs at the sink; now you have hairs everywhere and a disposable razor left on the side. We can combat this by disposing of the razor in the bin and keeping a microfiber cloth under our sink. A microfiber cloth should be used daily to wipe down the sink. We can also eliminate those nasty water marks on your shower doors by keeping a squeegee in the shower and wiping the water away. If you have shower curtains, you should consider washing them periodically, for instance, once a month. However, it's recommended that you replace it once or twice a year. Simple acts of tidying will completely revolutionize your bathroom, taking it from *Ugh, this room is disgusting* to *Wow, this room looks fantastic!*

## *Minimize Bacteria*

Minimizing clutter for a clean and calm environment really can mean executing some of the simplest tasks. For example, taking out the trash converts a dirty floor polluted by garbage into a clean, odorless room. Just like resisting the urge to throw wet towels or bath mats onto the ground will eliminate the likelihood of mold and mildew. If cleanliness is your top priority, then make sure to close the toilet lid before flushing. When we don't close the lid, we are inviting bacteria onto our countertops and floor, as toilet water will shoot out a fine mist that will travel throughout your bathroom. Speaking of bacteria, make sure to keep fresh hand towels and extra soap under your sink; this way, the next time you run out, you'll be able to grab a fresh bar or bottle without spreading bacteria.

## MINIMIZE DISTRACTIONS

### *Reduce Visual Stimuli*

We all enjoy decorating, adding those personal touches to your house to make it a home, and demonstrating your personality through different textures and colors. However, there are certain decorations that could be to your detriment and even heighten your ADHD symptoms. For example, the color of your walls can impact your day significantly: While neutral colors will emit a relaxing and positive atmosphere that can reduce stress and anxiety, colors that are bright and saturated, like red and yellow, will cause overstimulation and contribute to distraction. This can also be applied to the colors and patterns of our wall decorations and bath curtains. The ideal solution is opting for soft, muted colors.

Similar to decorations, lighting can cause overstimulation, subsequently affecting our ADHD symptoms. Harnessing natural light throughout the day will positively affect your mental health by improving productivity, focus, and sleep quality. In contrast, overexposure to artificial lighting can contribute to negative effects such as anxiety, stress, headaches, and visual discomfort. Nonetheless, it's almost impossible to avoid artificial lighting at night unless you take it back a few centuries and light some oil lamps. The optimal approach to avoiding the effects of artificial lighting is by using dim lamps or light bulbs to create a more relaxing environment.

Yet again, you've demonstrated your capability of achieving greatness. You have now redefined your bathroom by optimizing storage, decluttering, and establishing a creative cleaning schedule. Get ready to adore your new bathroom and the new visual techniques you can apply throughout your home. Remember, embrace your uniqueness; you've come this far because of it.

# BATHROOM CHECKLIST

This checklist is NOT meant to be completed in one day. Success comes through small consistent actions and not through big burnout sessions.

**Helpful tips:**

- STAY IN THE BATHROOM: Do not leave to re-home something until the bathroom is complete.
- Listen to music, books, or podcasts to make it fun.
- Adopt the minimalist mindset: be serious about getting rid of things that no longer serve you.

Identify pain points:
_____
_____

Set Realistic Goals:
_____
_____

Plan how you will overcome distraction and stay on task:
_____
_____

- [ ] Make sure you have your three boxes labeled *Re-home, Trash, and Donate.*

- [ ] Floor: pick up any trash, laundry, or items that do not belong in the bathroom.

- [ ] Counter: clear off everything from the counter and eliminate any items that do not have a purpose in the room. Disinfect the counter and sink, and return only the things that require frequent access.

- [ ] Toilet: eliminate any clutter sitting on or surrounding the toilet. Disinfect the inside and outside. Limit the number of items that get returned to this spot.

- [ ] Shower/bathtub: take everything out and spray with shower cleaner so it can soak while you sort the items. Throw away any unused or old soaps, razors, loofahs, etc. Scrub and rinse the shower/bathtub and return the items that are frequently used.

- [ ] Cabinets/drawers: go through one area at a time, removing everything that doesn't belong. Wipe down insides and surfaces. Return and organize everything based on its function and category.

- [ ] Plan a specific time each week to clean and tidy the bathroom so the organization is maintained: Day of week:_____ Time:_____

- [ ] Disperse the three boxes: throw away trash, drop-off donations, and re-home the items that did not belong in the bathroom.

## Inspire Others to Arrive and Open the Door to a Home that Gleams with Beauty

*"Remember that you are not alone. There are others going through the same thing."*

— ADAM LEVINE, LEAD SINGER OF MAROON 5

In the introduction, I spoke about how seemingly little things— like having a neat home and knowing where you've kept your keys, glasses, or wallet—can have a profound effect on your mood and well-being. By contrast, arriving home to a messy abode and feeling like you wouldn't know where to start can make you feel angry, frustrated, and despondent. This leads to procrastination and the avoidance of the inevitable.

It's all a rather ironic yet undeniable cycle. The bigger the mess gets, the less motivated you feel to clean it. The more it stresses you out, the easier it gets to "pretend like it doesn't exist." Yet clutter has the scientifically proven ability to put a dent in your happiness and self-esteem. What surrounds you is, in many ways, symbolic of how you feel about yourself, and my mission in writing this book is to ensure that what you see is bright, sparkling, and visually appealing. My hope is to inspire you to make your move little by little, setting bite-sized goals that make you feel increasingly motivated to keep the momentum going.

**By leaving a review of this book on Amazon, you'll show other readers with ADHD where they can find the informa-**

tion they need to have a home that everyone wants to come home to.

Simply by telling other readers how this book has helped you and what they'll find inside, you'll make it easy for them to find the vital tips and techniques that can make a big difference to their home enjoyment.

Thank you so much for your support. It means a lot to me that you're willing to help me give the practical, easy guidance that other readers crave, and I know it's going to make a difference. Now, let's get back on with it, shall we?

**Scan the QR code here**

# 6

# LAUNDRY

 *Movies kind of saved me from shame.*

— STEVEN SPIELBERG

Would you believe that one of the best directors of all time struggles to read? Battling judgment and fighting off bullies, Steven Spielberg grew up with dyslexia, learning to read two years later than his peers. Captivated by movies and harnessing them as a safe haven, Spielberg was not deterred. Instead, he tapped into his highest potential, becoming a true legend in the world of cinematics. Just as Steven Spielberg embraced his dyslexia, converting it into a source of empowerment, so can you on this journey to an elevated way of life.

## ASSESS YOUR LAUNDRY HABITS

### *Identify Pain Points*

Pick up dirty clothes, take them to the washing machine, separate colors, pour in detergent, select the appropriate wash, press start, wait till it finishes, then proceed to walk away and forget about it for the next few days. Yawn! Unfortunately, laundry is one of the most boring continuous tasks that we must complete to not smell like a trash can. While I can't promise to make laundry fun, I can provide you with solutions to ultimate laundry success, essentially making it easier and removing that dreaded feeling.

Firstly, you need to assess your laundry pain points. Ask yourself the following questions:

1. Do you procrastinate starting the laundry, constantly surviving off perfume and deodorant?
2. Is your laundry growing into a doom pile and becoming a more daunting task?
3. Are you confused about how to wash certain clothes?
4. Have you completely forgotten about the clothes in the washer or dryer?

### *Recognize Challenges*

Managing laundry is just as important as cleaning it. Personally, my biggest struggle was folding and organizing the clean laundry. Once a week, I'd muster up the motivation to start a wash so I didn't smell like a caveman at work, but somehow, the clothes would end up scattered across my bed, sofa, or even the floor. I'd justify myself, thinking, at least I don't smell bad; I'm not entering work with lint, dust, or questionable stains on my clothes, even if they are a bit wrinkly. I also had poor time management, and I would easily forget that I had left clean but wet clothes in my washing machine. By the time I realized a day or two later, they'd have a funky smell and wrinkles that were impossible to get out. When it comes to laundry, a lack of focus, time management, and motivation are often the common struggles.

### *Areas of Focus*

The only way we can create an improved way of living is by creating routines and prioritizing cleaning areas based on our own needs and not those of the masses. Take a look at your pain points and analyze where your focus is required. For instance, are you someone who forgets to even start the laundry? Do you procrastinate folding and hanging when the laundry is complete? A solution for this could be placing hangers from the clothes we've used in a basket. If we make sure to keep the basket in a visible spot, we can use it as a visual reminder to begin washing our clothes and to hang them back up once they're dry. Additionally, open storage is super beneficial, as it is a constant reminder to maintain an organized lifestyle.

## SORT AND DECLUTTER

### *How to Sort*

Don't you just hate how confusing laundry is? We have to sort by color and fabric to decide the temperature and spin cycle. While we all want to ignore these basic rules, keeping our clothes intact is a priority. The table below provides a guideline for the washing and drying cycles recommended for different types of fabric. This table will help you sort your dirty clothes into the correct categories.

**RECOMMENDED WASH AND DRY CYCLES**

| Fabric Type | Wash Cycle | Dry Cycle |
| --- | --- | --- |
| Cotton | Warm regular | Tumble dry, medium heat |
| Polyester | Warm regular or warm gentle | Tumble dry, low heat |
| Linen | Warm regular/hot | Tumble dry, low heat, or hang dry |
| Denim | Cold regular | Tumble dry, low heat, or hang dry |
| Synthetic | Cold gentle or dry clean | Tumble dry, low heat, or lay flat |
| Silk | Cold gentle, handwash, or dry clean | Lay flat |
| Wool | Cold gentle, handwash, or dry clean | Lay flat |
| Cashmere | Dry clean | Dry clean |
| Garments with intricate embellishments | Dry clean | Dry clean |

These are general recommendations for washing and drying certain fabrics, but always check your tags for more specific cleaning instructions. For mixed materials, just follow the recommendations for the highest percentage of material. For example, if a t-shirt is 25% polyester and 75% cotton, then follow the rules of cleaning cotton. Additionally, particularly stinky items can be washed with hot water to kill the bacteria, but be sure to select a gentle or regular cycle based on the fabric type.

*Special Care Items*

Naturally, delicate clothing is quite confusing, and the name alone makes you question if you should wash it at all. Like normal clothing, delicates can also be placed in the washing machine, though some people prefer to wash them by hand. In both cases, you begin by sorting color and material, turning the clothing inside out, and ensuring the zippers are fully closed to prevent any tears. Make sure to hand wash any stains before placing them in the washing machine (the table below lists a variety of home remedies that can be used to remove stains). Next, place the delicate in your mesh washing bag and add your detergent. Select the gentle or delicate setting, and soon enough, you'll have clean clothes.

Delicate clothing is extremely susceptible to losing its shape if not dried correctly. Swap out the dryer for a clean white towel and lay it flat on a surface. Place your delicates on top and wait for the water to be absorbed. Proceed by hanging them to air dry; this may take a day, depending on the weather. Don't forget to add a reminder to your phone or diary so you can come back the following day to organize them in your closet.

## HOME REMEDIES FOR STAIN REMOVAL

| Type of Stain | Stain Remover (pre-wash) | Wash Temperature |
|---|---|---|
| Oil, grease, or makeup | Liquid dish soap | Warm/hot water |
| Dirt or clay | Pre-soak in detergent water | Warm water for set stains Cold water for fresh stains |
| Blood or sweat | Hydrogen peroxide or pre-soak in cold water | Cold water |
| Ink or dye | Rubbing alcohol or milk | Cold water |
| Wine, tea, or coffee | White vinegar or club soda | Cold water |
| Grass | White vinegar or rubbing alcohol | Cold water |
| Tomato | Baking soda paste or lemon juice | Cold water |

### Declutter

Your laundry area should not be a place for junk that accumulates in your house. There shouldn't be a pile of mismatched socks or a collection of empty detergent containers on top of your machines. We often forget things in the pockets of our pants, such as loose change, tissues, or receipts. When we discover these things, we end up dumping them on any available surface in the room. This is added clutter that we must find a home for; we could use a specific box for these random items and relocate them to their designated homes once a week. This gives these items a temporary home and eliminates the scattered mess.

### Establish Zones

Creating designated spaces for items allows for clean and happy homes. Hampers are easily overloaded; I recommend allocating an individual laundry basket to each member of the family and keeping it in their bedroom. This way, it prevents one communal hamper from overflowing every other day in the laundry room. Nonetheless, there should be an allocated hamper in the laundry room for sheets, towels, and extra dirty items. Additionally, it is paramount that laundry detergent is stored high and away from children or pets. It is best kept in the laundry room on a shelf, cabinet, or storage cart, along with dryer sheets and other laundry essentials.

## WASHING AND DRYING

### Create a Schedule

The first step to our new laundry routine is investing in hampers with multiple sections; this will save you time when it comes to sorting dirty clothes. Next, we need to schedule our washing, drying, and folding time. For example, on Monday, you complete three sessions of washing, drying, and folding— one session at breakfast, the second session at lunchtime, and the third at dinner time. Usually, washers and dryers have built-in alarms that will beep when they have finished their job. If you're anything like me, you're usually stuck in multiple tasks at once and probably won't even hear the alarm. To combat this, we can set a timer on our phones and place it in an area that is within reach. This way, if we are in the middle of another task, we can hit the snooze button multiple times to remind us of the laundry. Once we're ready, we can proceed to fulfilling our laundry routine. By allocating set times and days to washing and folding, you will avoid stressing over what items you don't have clean or can't find. In addition, we should keep an eye on the laundry detergent and dryer sheets; the last thing we want is to get to laundry day and realize we have run out of supplies.

### Tips and Tricks

Maximizing the use of our laundry appliances won't only save you time but also money on that energy bill. Even the simplest of hacks can prevent you from running another cycle on the washing machine, such as throwing your socks into a mesh bag and tossing them into the next load of washing. You can even add a color catcher to prevent any sneaky colors from leaking, and the mesh bag prevents the machine from swallowing the socks. Furthermore, if you leave the washing machine door open after every wash, you'll prevent mold and smelly odors, freeing up more of your time.

## Set Reminders

Our ADHD can prevent us from feeling motivated if we don't enjoy the activity, so why not make laundry a game between you and your family? Alarms are the best way for us to know when a washing or drying load has finished; thus, the idea of the game is to beat the clock. Both you and a member of your family set the exact same alarm; once the alarm goes off, the first one to the laundry room can skip folding their laundry. It's a fun and competitive game that aims to relieve the stress of the provider or family member who is usually stuck with all household responsibilities. So, set your alarms and get running!

## FOLD AND STORE

As we have learned, we must hang or fold our clothing as soon as it has finished drying. However, there are certain tips and tricks to save you from folding annoying items like towels and sheets. When it comes to bedding, the best approach is to put them straight back onto the bed once they're clean. Keep a few extra sheets for guests or emergencies, but any more than three pairs can be considered additional clutter. Avoid folding towels and try rolling them; it's a great way to save space in your linen closet, and they are less likely to become a huge mess. Additionally, don't waste your time attempting to fold underwear, socks, or tiny children's clothes when they can all be laid flat in a drawer.

### Share Responsibility

No one likes being the one responsible for folding an entire family's clean laundry; hence, family members and even children must be included. An excellent method for achieving this is by investing in multiple plastic laundry baskets that are only used for clean linen. Each member will have a label with their name on the basket. When it's time, the family can take the baskets and begin folding and organizing their clothes into their own closets.

### Storage Solutions

Laundry has made me basket crazy; it is a tool that provides easy access, keeps my folded clothes wrinkle-free, and is super versatile. Two or three wicker baskets that can slide in and out of your closet seamlessly are a super handy storage solution for those who don't have a chest of drawers. It will keep clothes neatly folded and can be used to separate shirts from pants. Additionally, hanging shelves are a super affordable option that can provide you with folding freedom and function as a closet divider.

### The Sock Dilemma

If you're anything like me, you've asked yourself multiple times where your missing socks are while staring at a pile of single socks. To implement sock management, we first need to purge all the singles and throw them into a tote bag. This can be done by collecting all your socks, placing them in a clear space, and matching them. The singles can then be placed in the tote and hung in your laundry room. The next time you can't find the mate to your sock, simply look in your tote bag, and it should be there.

Sometimes, having a set of drawers is not enough to keep socks tidy. Sock organizers are total life savers for drawers that have no built-in storage. They consist of multiple rows of slots that are the perfect size for your feet warmers and prevent absolute chaos within your drawer. Not to mention, they're super affordable.

*Maintenance Habits*

While the primary goal of doing laundry is to prevent dirt and grime on our linen, we also need to prevent it in the room where we wash our linen. Habits like cleaning up laundry detergent spills and immediately recycling bottles are super important. We also need to place items back where they belong immediately after use. On your laundry days, include a wipe-down of all surfaces to avoid the buildup of powders, detergents, and dust. It would be a waste to accidentally place fresh clothes on a dirty countertop.

Well done for using your ADHD as a source of empowerment. You now understand and have the ability to implement efficient laundry washing, drying, and folding techniques and routines. From decluttering to organizing, you have managed to save yourself copious amounts of time and energy, making laundry more manageable than ever. In the following chapter, we'll be conquering the garage chaos.

# LAUNDRY CHECKLIST

This checklist is NOT meant to be completed in one day. Success comes through small consistent actions and not through big burnout sessions.

**Helpful tips:**

- STAY IN THE LAUNDRY ROOM: Do not leave to re-home something until the room is complete.
- Listen to music, books, or podcasts to make it fun.
- Adopt the minimalist mindset: be serious about getting rid of things that no longer serve you.

Identify pain points:
_____
_____

Set Realistic Goals:
_____
_____

Plan how you will overcome distraction and stay on task:
_____
_____

☐ Make sure you have your three boxes labeled *Re-home, Trash, and Donate.*

☐ Collect all the dirty laundry throughout the house, including dish rags, towels, and rugs.

☐ Sort the laundry into categories based on fabric material: cotton, polyester, heavy duty, whites, delicates, etc.

☐ Floors: pick up any trash, old clothes or rags, and random items that need a home. Sort into boxes.

☐ Surfaces: remove everything from the tops of the machines, tables, and countertops. Wipe down the surfaces. Sort any misplaced items into their respective boxes and return anything that belongs in the room.

☐ Cabinets/shelves: remove everything and sort any misplaced items in this area. Wipe down. Return and organize items that belong in this room into categories: cleaning supplies, laundry items, towels, etc.

☐ Wash: start a load in the washer and set a timer to remind you to move the clothes to the dryer.

☐ Dry: move clothes to the dryer and begin a new wash in the washer. Set a timer for when the drying is done.

☐ Remember to keep cycling the current loads of laundry and fold them right away to avoid another DOOM pile.

☐ Plan a specific time each week to clean and tidy the laundry room and wash, dry, and put away your clothes: Day of week:_____ Time:_____

☐ Disperse the three boxes: throw away trash, drop-off donations, and re-home the items that did not belong in the laundry room

# 7

# GARAGE

My head was always up, looking beyond the classroom, daydreaming. I didn't want to ask the teacher for help, not again, anyway. I always had my hand up and was slower than everybody else; why doesn't anyone else ask questions? How do they know what to do when I don't? I just didn't get it. I wanted to be like everyone else and not get called a dummy and laughed at.

I would think: *I'm just going to sit here and wait until the teacher notices I'm not doing anything. Yeah, that's what I'll do. I'll wait. But she's reading a book now. Half the class is over, and I haven't written anything. I don't want to hand in a blank piece of paper, so I'll pretend like I'm completely clueless.*

"Don't be afraid to ask for help and admit when you need it," is what my teacher said to me the following week. Another ungraded test paper, and I was failing. But my fear of regular ridicule and embarrassment was always greater than my fear of failing the class—at least I only had to deal with one dose of shame at the end of the year. Neurodivergence is still not accepted in our education system and is often named "special needs." When are the high focus, deep intensity of work, and an alternative way of working going to be celebrated as superpowers rather than shamed for being different from the norm?

I was shocked to find that Charles Schwab, a stock market tycoon, had a similar experience in the classroom. I've always found numbers fascinating, so knowing that another neurodivergent individual like me could revolutionize something as important as the stock market became one of my biggest inspirations.

## ASSESS YOUR GARAGE

### Identify Pain Points

The garage, also known as the storage sanctuary, offers refuge to a million and one sentimental items I've collected over the years. Whether it's tools, bikes, boxes, or furniture, the garage is the one room that is slightly acceptable to have a reasonable amount of clutter. However, a few boxes here and there can quickly become a haven for trash. Let's dive straight in and assess where the fundamental problems in your garage are:

- Are boxes stacked too high? Perhaps you can never reach something when you need it.
- Do you have rodents festering in the trash and now moving on to your precious belongings?

- Are you unable to park your car inside due to the amount of clutter?
- Do you have enough storage and shelving?

Recognize the issue and make a note of it.

### Distraction is Inevitable

One of the biggest difficulties we'll encounter when cleaning the garage is staying focused. Unlike other rooms where we find the items that don't belong and make new homes for them, the garage usually holds keepsakes, random household supplies, and even Christmas decorations. This means there's a multitude of opportunities for us to get distracted. With the strategies we learned in Chapter 2, we can overcome distractions and our inability to focus. Develop a plan for how you will combat distraction, stay focused, and be productive. Plan for the inevitable and decide beforehand what you will do in a distracting scenario.

### Set Realistic Goals

To convert our trash haven into an organized sanctuary, it's necessary that we have a vision for what we want from our garage. Thus, we begin our journey in the garage by setting goals. Without a goal, we might just leave our garage in a worse state than it was already in. Our goals are often based on individual preference, so to make this easier, think back to the pain point and find a solution. For example, if you're sick and tired of having to find a parking space on the street because your garage is at maximum capacity, then your primary goal is going to be optimizing storage to create the perfect space for your vehicle.

## CLEAR THE CLUTTER

Now that we have a goal in mind let's begin removing obvious trash, such as soda cans, empty paint tins, and broken glass. This is the perfect time to remove anything that does not belong in your garage; maybe you have an over-spilling box of recycling or wine bottles. These two steps should have created a clear floor, allowing you to move freely and safely without any tripping hazards.

After we have relocated items that don't belong, we must create sections within the garage. Each shelving area should have its own section, separate sections for tools, outdoor gear, gardening, and more. Grab a pen and paper and write down each section. Imagine it as a mini checklist. Find some trash bags or cardboard boxes to label "trash," "donate," and "sell." While it's great that we're decluttering, we should also be mindful of what we're throwing away. They do say one man's trash is another man's treasure. Moreover, forget tackling the whole garage at once and begin section by section, clearing clutter into calm and ticking off your checklist. We can't expect ourselves to get everything done in one day; if we take small, consistent steps, we are more likely to achieve our goal.

## Sort and Categorize

Sorting items into categories will allow us to stay organized long-term, and we'll be able to know exactly where everything is. Start by making the categories broad and not too detailed. Microorganizing can be too specific and demanding, especially when attempting big tasks. This means that all tools are grouped together, just like Halloween and Christmas decorations can be placed together, as well as sports equipment with the paddling pool. They are defined yet simple categories: tools, decorations, and sports.

## Learn to Let Go

Inevitably, we are all going to come across items that are difficult to part with. Personally, I have the habit of fully investing in new hobbies such as candle making and losing interest within a week. I'll buy all the equipment to have it end up in my garage, collecting dust for the next few years. Though items like these have a great idea behind them, we've often moved on and no longer need them. With that in mind, if you find your brain convincing yourself to keep an item you haven't touched in a long time, consider putting it in the donate or sell box. The same rule can be applied to sentimental belongings; we all love a trip down memory lane, but not when so many memorable boxes block your car from entering the garage. Don't let the past block you from the present.

## MAXIMIZE STORAGE

Pegboards are one of my favorite tools for organizing versatile spaces; they allow you to change the organization of a shelf just by adding different hooks in different places. They're also perfect for hanging tools you might need in a rush, such as a wrench if your faucet starts flooding the house. Shelving units and cabinets are optimal for garages because they have built-in storage. Avoid using cardboard boxes as they can grow mold and become a habitat for insects. If you're looking for the ultimate storage solution, it doesn't get much better than overhead storage racks. An overhead storage rack is a shelf that is installed into the ceiling of your garage, holding multiple bins, which is perfect for those seasonal items we don't use often. It allows more space on the ground, and it's unnoticeable unless you're looking up at the ceiling.

### Establish Zones

It's time to stop using your garage as a dumping ground and start creating a home for every item. While we have established sections in our garage, we need to consider if they're allowing us to take full advantage of the room. Chunky toolboxes, big lawnmowers, and gardening supplies are often the culprits for leaving no empty space. Grab a pen and paper and have a little doodling session to create designated zones and find the best way to store your big items. Keep in mind that it's important to store dirty garden supplies away from food storage and gym equipment. Perhaps store gardening supplies on hooks, while on the opposite wall, you can stack water-resistant boxes for your camping gear. Food should be stored off the ground to avoid pests, so consider a shelving unit for this.

## Labeling System

Labels help you quickly identify where an item is. This means you won't spend hours digging through multiple boxes and causing a huge mess that you'll be too tired to clean up. For this reason, grab your sticky labels and pen to enhance long-term organizational results and reduce stress. While labeling, you should also stack boxes in a logical order. Place what you're least likely to use at the bottom of the stack and most likely to use at the top. This way, when you need an item from the garage, it'll be easily accessible and within reach.

## CREATE WORKSTATIONS

### Organize for Function

Garages are extremely versatile spaces; they enable us to build new things, complete a workout, and partake in some gardening all in one room. Thus, it's crucial we create areas that facilitate these activities by designating specific zones. For those of us who love to build or complete DIY projects, a convertible worktable will ensure you'll always have room to get creative. You could also create a workout zone with storage for mats, weights, and a speaker so you can exercise without leaving home. A gardening zone would have shelves for seeds, tools, and knee pads, making indoor and outdoor planting effortless. Consider installing a coat rack and cubbies for mittens, hats, and shoes to keep seasonal items organized. You could even create a food storage area with a freezer and shelves to preserve ingredients and reduce trips to the grocery store. With mindful zoning, the garage operates as a functional space for hobbies, health, and household needs. Get creative with how you use this versatile room.

## Lighting Considerations

Unlike other rooms, garages usually have the worst lighting in the entire house, as they're not intended to be used for anything other than parking a car. In contrast to spaces like our bathroom and bedroom, where dim lighting enhances a positive and relaxing atmosphere, the garage needs bright artificial light. Placing them directly over your DIY station is optimal for avoiding nasty injuries. Whereas, if the lighting source is behind you, you'll have shadows blocking your view. Bear in mind that long periods of exposure can cause increased stress on our ADHD brain and lead to overstimulation.

## STREAMLINE SEASONAL STORAGE

### Rotate Seasonal Items

Implementing a systematic approach to rotating seasonal items, such as decorations and car tires, takes organization to a whole new level. Not only will you have easy access to your items once the seasons change, but you'll also be enhancing your clutter-free environment. Creating a rotational system involves organizing the selected items by season, starting with the season that's approaching and descending in order. Label storage containers or even tag dates to racks and shelves. This way, you'll know exactly when to begin rotating. You can also make a note of it on your physical calendar or set a phone reminder. During the rotating process, assess items like tires for wear and tear and decorations for mold or insects.

*Proper Storage Strategies*

Sports play a significant role in our lives, whether for our kids or ourselves; it's majorly beneficial to our mental and social interactions. It only makes sense that we dedicate a well-organized and clean portion of our house to it. Naturally, this is often the garage. Start the organizing process by going through all your equipment and checking if it still works. For instance, are there any holes or tears in footballs or basketballs? For any duplicates that you no longer want or need, you can donate or pass them on to a friend. Next, we need to select an area of our walls or floor that'll be dedicated to sports. Proceeding this, you'll have to choose your method of organization; this could be baskets for balls and hooks for rackets.

Imagine you've just arrived at a beautiful camping site; the kids are excited, and you are eager to get out your expensive camping equipment. Once it's all set up, it begins to rain, so you and the kids huddle inside the tent, but oh no, there are multiple tears and holes where the water starts leaking into the tent. At this moment, you realize with a few simple storage solutions, you could have easily prevented this. The key is finding a cool, dry place at home to store all your camping equipment together when not in use. Avoid cramming gear into a damp garage or attic. Instead, dedicate space in a cabinet, closet, or basement. This prevents mildew and damage from temperature fluctuations.

Carefully pack tents, sleeping bags, and pads to avoid tearing fragile fabrics and bending tent poles. Roll up and fasten with ties rather than stuffing into a bag. Use clear plastic bins to corral smaller items like flashlights, bug spray, camp stoves, and utensils. Labeling makes grabbing gear a breeze. And don't forget the food! Seal non-perishables in airtight containers to keep out moisture and pests. With mindful storage between trips, you'll have quality camping gear ready for years of future adventures. No more ruined trips from damaged, disorganized equipment.

Who doesn't love Christmas, Halloween, and Easter? Holidays are everyone's favorite time of the year; they allow us a mini escape, a pause in everyday life, to embrace memorable moments while sharing love and tradition with our family. We want to make sure that mold and mildew don't ruin the decorations for these holiday seasons. The most effective way to conserve decorations is water-resistant plastic containers. It's also ideal if you choose neutral-colored boxes and use labels or color-code the bins according to which holiday decorations they hold. Remember to stack them and seasonally rotate them for efficiency.

## ESTABLISH ROUTINES

Unlike busy living spaces, our garage isn't used as frequently and thus doesn't need as much regular maintenance to stay clean and tidy. You should allocate roughly one hour a month to maintain your organized garage. Choose one day and begin by taking a look around and ensuring everything is stored in its assigned box. Proceed by wiping down surfaces, shelves, and workbenches to prevent dust build-up. You can finish the job by sweeping and mopping the floor. In the end, you should have a tidy and clean garage to be proud of.

### *Maintenance Habits*

Tidying up after projects and activities is as simple as putting things back where they came from. After everything is back in its place, make sure all trash is thrown away, and any dirty surfaces are wiped down. Establishing simple yet effective habits will prevent you from spending agonizing amounts of time on decluttering and deep cleaning. Even when your ADHD symptoms are screaming at you to complete the clean-up at a later time, stick to it and persevere.

Successfully implementing these strategies means you have conquered the garage chaos. Now, you have a revolutionized space that fits your car, is perfect for a multitude of hobbies, and meets all your storage needs. Next, get ready to boost your productivity in the office.

# GARAGE CHECKLIST

This checklist is NOT meant to be completed in one day. Success comes through small consistent actions and not through big burnout sessions.

**Helpful tips:**

- STAY IN THE GARAGE.
- Listen to music, books, or podcasts to make it fun.
- Adopt the minimalist mindset: be serious about getting rid of things that no longer serve you.

Identify pain points:

_____

_____

Set Realistic Goals:

_____

_____

Plan how you will overcome distraction and stay on task:

_____

_____

☐ Designate zones: grab a pencil and paper and map out different areas in the garage for specific functions. Examples include: gardening, exercise, workbench/tools, storage, parking, etc.

☐ Make sure you have your three boxes labeled *Re-home, Trash, and Donate/Sell.*

**\*Relocate and disperse the obvious things that don't belong here before continuing. This will allow for a clear space to work in and reduce negative stimulation.**

☐ Workbenches: remove everything off these surfaces and dust or wipe them down. Sort any items that do not belong into the labeled boxes. Return items to these surfaces based on category. Remember some of these items will find new homes as you continue to reorganize the garage as a whole.

☐ Shelves: remove everything from the shelves and dust or wipe down. Sort any items that do not belong into the labeled boxes. Return items to these shelves making sure that frequently used items are more accessible.

☐ Boxes/bins: go through each box/bin one at a time. Get rid of anything that you haven't used within the last year. Make sure that these boxes/bins have designated categories: holiday decor, camping gear, sports, home projects, etc. Don't mix categories.

☐ Tools: go through toolboxes and organize drawers and compartments based on function. For example: wrenches, screwdrivers, hammers, sockets, hardware, powertools, etc.

☐ Outdoor equipment: designate a space to hang and store seasonal yard tools. These include: winter shovels, rakes, gardening items, lawnmower, weed wacker, hoses, etc. Ensure accessibility for the current season's tools.

☐ Automotive: designate a safe shelf space for various automotive items. These include: oil, filters, fluids, lights, tires, jackstands, etc.

☐ Exercise equipment: if you have gym equipment, dust it off and designate enough space for safe use and easy access. If a gym is not part of your garage, be sure that sports equipment like bicycles, balls, rackets, and hoops have space to be stored on hooks and shelves.

☐ Floors: once everything has a designated place and has been put away properly, the floors should be clear. Give them a thorough sweep.

☐ Plan a specific time each month to tidy the garage and rotate any seasonal items so the organization is maintained: Day of the month:_____ Time:_____

☐ Disperse the three boxes: throw away trash, drop-off donations, and re-home the items that did not belong in the garage.

# 8

# OFFICE

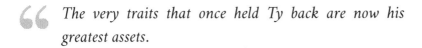
*The very traits that once held Ty back are now his greatest assets.*

— MOTHER OF TY PENNINGTON

Ty Pennington, the home improvement expert, was quite an active kid. From swinging around naked on classroom curtains to having explosive feelings that felt as if they were holding his body hostage, he assumed he was just different from everyone else with no real reason why. While his peers had their heads down furiously writing and studying, he was bursting with energy, confused and burdened as to what was wrong with his brain. After years of giving everyone around him heart attacks and great shocks, he decided to seek help in college, finally being given an answer to what made him so unique. At last, his ADHD diagnosis allowed him to see, and putting on a fresh pair of glasses with shiny new lenses brought clarity to everything. Ty was no longer an academic failure who sought attention from his peers by acting recklessly but a boy who had triumphed over the adversities and trials of ADHD and transcended. ADHD is a powerful source of distinctive capabilities, not a liability.

## ASSESS YOUR OFFICE

### Identify Pain Points

Let's face it: Your office setup probably has an extended list of frustrating and annoying aspects that not only prevent you from getting work done but also hinder your ability to excel. So, let's say goodbye to mediocrity and hello to a revolutionized office by expelling these pain points. Let's answer the following questions:

- What frustrates you most about your working environment?
- Are you constantly distracted by noise and unable to put pen to paper?
- Can you find the necessary resources to start work? Such as your laptop charger, which is probably amid a cluster of other wires.
- Does your desk or chair cause back or neck pain?
- Do you have heaps of unorganized paperwork?

While working from home has its advantages, it can come with many distractions. Our objective is to eradicate these disturbances and create the ultimate work environment.

*Recognize Challenges*

Some of the primary obstacles that those with ADHD must overcome are clutter and distraction. Both challenges usually walk hand in hand due to the fact that a messy environment equals a messy mind. An office for someone with a neurodivergent brain typically consists of mounts of unorganized paperwork, empty coffee cups, wrappers sprawled across the desk, and multiple doom piles of random household items. I'm sure you've also attempted to sporadically stick Post-it notes to remind you of everything you need to do, ultimately forgetting because it's now one huge mess. In turn, this leaves you with brain fog and struggling to accomplish your work.

*Set Realistic Goals*

Now is the moment for you to leave that clutter behind and imagine an office that allows you to flourish and prevail. What do you see in this vision?

Grab a notepad and pen and write down ideas that will bring this vision to life. Maybe your workspace is color-coded with organized paperwork. Are you finally able to sit down at your desk and jump straight into work without rummaging through boxes and untangling wires? Clarify your dream and goals for this room, as you will need a clear picture to make it a reality.

## DECLUTTER YOUR WORKSPACE

Organizing can feel stressful and overwhelming, especially when there are piles of paperwork involved. Hence, we will break down the office decluttering into more approachable steps. Begin by removing obvious trash, such as old food, tissues, or coffee cups. Then, move on to removing everything from your desk drawers and cabinets. Make sure to grab those old cardboard boxes from the garage and put them to use by labeling them "keep" and "throw." For paperwork that is confusing and can't be allocated into a binder at this moment, place it in the keep box for another day. It's important not to overwhelm ourselves. Thoroughly disinfect your desk area and begin placing items back inside your desk while labeling and creating designated places. You should now have a clean slate to organize binders, paperwork, and office supplies.

### *Sort and Categorize*

Mess and clutter become boring and tiring fast, meaning it's vital we sort our office supplies adequately to prevent a repetitive cycle. First, let's separate our office accessories, such as pens, pencils, and Post-it notes, from random papers and files. All these items need their own categories and designated space; they should not be compiled into one big group. Now that they're separated place the pens, paper clips, and traditional office accessories away in an empty container for later. Proceed by dividing random utility bills from work projects, placing each in its own pile. Subsequently, you can categorize your files, for instance, data reports into one group and financial reports in another. Lastly, place them in labeled containers so they stay tidy.

## Minimize Distractions

Making effective use of our office means banishing all unnecessary clutter and distractions to harness productivity and concentration, enabling us to thrive. Clutter isn't always just junk or mounts of papers; it can also be picture frames of your family, comfy blankets and pillows that make you feel tired, or even over-stimulating colors. Instead of throwing these items away, consider finding a new home for them, somewhere that doesn't prioritize focus. Simplicity is key when it comes to our office.

## STREAMLINE STORAGE

### Storage Solutions

Integrating storage into our offices will effectively boost our productivity and focus. A personal favorite is bookshelves; they are an affordable way to add height and avoid taking up surplus amounts of floor room. Not only do they store files and books where I can see them, but they also allow for fabric bins to be placed and labeled. For those who love open organization, they are the ideal investment. However, if you prefer to have your office materials hidden and out of the way, consider rolling carts or file cabinets. Both options are sleek and smooth ways to categorize and maintain a tidy workspace.

## *Establish Zones*

Your desk should always be a home for simple office supplies. For instance, you can use desktop utensil holders to store your favorite pens, pencils, and sticky notes. This ensures that the next time you make an appointment or are on a phone call, you'll have pens at hand to write down the date or information. Mail, receipts, and utility bills are usually the first ones to get lost in piles of paper. Combat this by installing a wall organization rack; it will keep the random yet vital pieces of paper stored safely. Reference materials are naturally bulky and consume a significant amount of room; thus, it is necessary that we dedicate a large portion of storage to them. In the previous section, we discussed bookshelves. This would be an ideal location to house referencing material. Never forget that every item in your house deserves a designated place.

## *Labeling System*

Labels are exceptionally beneficial in an office environment, enabling easy retrieval and clarity. A color-coding system will be your best friend when it comes to filing and categorizing paperwork. Start by placing your least used files at the back of your cabinet, working your way forward with more frequently used paperwork. This will allow swift accessibility to the documents you're most likely to use. Additionally, for the files that are in current use, you're going to need colored tabs, specifically red, yellow, and green. The traffic light system uses red as urgent paperwork, whereas yellow isn't quite as important, and green will symbolize that you still have time to work on it.

Thus, even on days when you forget to write down your important work tasks and just can't seem to remember, you'll have the answers right in front of you in a systematic order.

## DIGITAL ORGANIZATION

### Digital Decluttering Techniques

Just as we have decluttered our physical space, we should also clear out our virtual environment. Start by unsubscribing to email lists and articles you don't read or like anymore. This is unnecessary clutter that is filling up your email. You can clear out your spam box and create folders for different types of important emails. For example, when you receive receipts via email, you'll be able to store them all in one place, which is super handy if you need to return something. If you're feeling unmotivated to begin this task, bear in mind that deleting emails contributes to reducing carbon dioxide emissions, effectively saving plants and trees.

### Computer Organization

While we have already organized and sorted our old files and paperwork, we can prevent such a tiring task in the future. This can be done by creating labeled files on our laptops and computers. Essentially, it is the same as how you would label a physical file, but without extensive work or copious amounts of time. You simply create a new file on your laptop and begin saving electronic versions of utility bills or financial papers.

## Utilize Cloud Storage

Naturally, when we come across important documents or information, we feel the need to print it off and store it somewhere safe. However, years and years of this continuous cycle can build a tremendous amount of clutter when there is actually a super simple solution. Cloud storage is a provider on our laptops and phones that enables us to store and save data and files. If you have any Apple products, the service should be built in, but other companies and apps like Google Drive or Dropbox provide the same function. Cloud storage is the way of the future, saving you from a house full of messy paperwork.

## OPTIMIZE WORKFLOW

Whether you have a big or small desk, its arrangement and setup are crucial for productivity. Simplicity is key in terms of what is placed on your desk; avoid overcrowding and be selective. Ask yourself if you really need that fake plant or picture frame taking up all that space. Additionally, create a designated area for personal items that you might need during work hours, such as tissues and lip balm. Preferably, keep a small trash can by your feet or under your desk to dispose of unwanted papers and tissues throughout the day. This will prevent the mess from accumulating on your desk. Consider investing in a cable box to keep monitor wires secure and laptop chargers untangled.

If comfort is a priority to you and your busy work schedule, then investing in a chair that is both supportive and soft is crucial. A desk chair should provide lumbar support, allow your feet to rest flat on the floor, and have armrests. If you work in front of a monitor, ensure it is steadily placed at eye level to prevent neck strains and back pain. Lighting should also be considered; be sure to reduce or increase screen brightness based on your visual sensitivity.

TIME MANAGEMENT

*Plan for Success*

Planners are the perfect tool to get a head start on your day; imagine waking up and having already planned what task needs completing and when. If we allocate time every evening to sit down and plan the following day, it will take the stress away from the moment at hand and allow for mental clarity. Planning our days in advance doesn't just mean work; it's important that we also schedule our appointments, mealtimes, and responsibilities. Begin by organizing your days in thirty-minute increments, allowing for flexibility and unplanned situations. Additionally, task management apps, such as Google Tasks, will keep you consistent and allow you to share your progress with others.

*Improve Focus*

While planning, labeling, and writing sticky notes are all huge helpers, we also need further strategies that are specifically tailored to our ADHD brains and symptoms. Our working memory deficit often means that mentally calculating and visualizing how much time we need for a task can be almost impossible. The solution to this is time blocking in a way that allows us to visualize urgency.

Begin by making a list of all the tasks you need and want to complete. Then, we can apply the traffic light system once again, highlighting tasks in red if they need to be completed this week, yellow if they need to be done this month, and green if they don't have a due date. Now that we have ordered our tasks by color coding, we can place the yellow and red ones in our planner. Green tasks can be moved to a separate list or document for goals for the year. Make sure to tick off the tasks as you go and check back in weekly to see what hasn't been completed.

## MANAGE DISTRACTIONS

*Eliminate the Social Itch*

Social media, Facebook, Instagram, and TV are the leading auditory and visual distractions in our day-to-day lives. Even though the majority of things we see and hear about have zero correlation to our work, it can be hard to resist the urge to open up your own phone and have a quick browse. Over time, this slowly becomes a habit, and you find yourself picking your phone up more and more just to have a look, ultimately leaving your office feeling unaccomplished and stressed about the following day's workload. While you won't want to hear this, the best solution is to leave your phone outside of the office. If you need your phone for work or emergencies and are unable to leave it in another room, consider silencing notifications from distracting apps. You could even set limits on some of them so you are not tempted to use them during work hours.

### Establish Boundaries

Whether it's our family or colleagues, interruptions are a daily occurrence. However, unlike neurotypical individuals, it's harder for us to get back on track once we've been distracted. Setting boundaries means that you, your family, or a colleague still get to have that important conversation, just at a later time when it's more convenient for you and your attention. When you are interrupted, take a look at your planner and establish a good time when you won't require focus. Try saying, "I would really like to discuss this with you, but I really need to get this task completed. Could we talk later today at 5 p.m.?"

### Enhance Focus

Noise-canceling headphones are the ultimate tool for drowning out excessive background noise. If your office is chaotic and simply shutting the door doesn't work, then think about purchasing a decent pair of headphones to tap into your deep focus.

The next time you sit in your office, I recommend you look around and admire your tremendous effort to create a beautifully organized and productive work environment. These organizational techniques have given you the opportunity to excel like never before in your job. Just like Ty Pennington, you harnessed your ADHD symptoms, making them a true asset. In the following chapter, we'll be reinventing our family's shared haven, the living room.

# OFFICE CHECKLIST

This checklist is NOT meant to be completed in one day. Success comes through small consistent actions and not through big burnout sessions.

**Helpful tips:**

- STAY IN THE OFFICE: Do not leave to re-home something until the room is complete.
- Listen to music, books, or podcasts to make it fun.
- Adopt the minimalist mindset: be serious about getting rid of things that no longer serve you.

Identify pain points:

_____

_____

Set Realistic Goals:

_____

_____

Plan how you will overcome distraction and stay on task:

_____

_____

☐ Make sure you have your three boxes labeled *Re-home, Trash, and Donate.*

☐ Desk: clear everything off the desk and give it a good wipe down. As you return items to the desk, be honest about the items that no longer serve you or that contribute to overstimulation. This room's function is focus; shape the environment accordingly

☐ Shelves: clear shelves of knick-knacks, files, and office supplies. Dust off the shelves and sort items by category, eliminating anything that doesn't belong.

☐ Filing cabinets: go through cabinets one drawer at a time. Designate a category for each drawer. Utilize labels and tabs for easy access to important documents. Throw away or shred old documents.

☐ Wires: utilize wire boxes or ties to create a neat workspace and remove the eye sore that can lead to overstimulation and tripping hazards.

☐ Digital declutter: create and designate file locations on your devices for digital files. This will eliminate much of the physical documents in your office, and allow for quick access when you need to find something. Go through emails, receipts, taxes, downloads, photos, etc.

☐ Decor: assess which knick-knacks and photos set the mood for focus, and which ones are distracting. Less is more when it comes to your office.

☐ Disperse the three boxes: throw away trash, drop-off donations, and re-home the items that did not belong in the office.

☐ Every time you use your office, allow yourself 5 minutes to put documents in their designated places and clean up your desk.

# 9

# LIVING ROOM

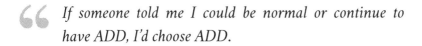 *If someone told me I could be normal or continue to have ADD, I'd choose ADD.*

— DAVID NEELEMAN

Creativity, passion, and dedication are all symptoms of ADHD that led David Neeleman to become an international airline success. The CEO of JetBlue Airlines utilized his inability to focus, procrastination, and disorganization to think outside of the box, unleashing a new age of aviation and travel. Much like planes, those of us with ADHD also experience turbulence, constantly facing disruptions and challenges. Ultimately, we land in a completely new destination, one filled with knowledge and compassion, and we take control of our own destiny.

## ASSESS YOUR LIVING ROOM

### Identify Pain Points

Our Living room is a communal space for the entire family. This means it's a high-traffic area, leading to the constant influx of items and belongings being traipsed in and out. Ultimately, we end up with random piles of socks, toys, and papers everywhere, while the one thing we desperately want, the remote control, is nowhere to be found. So, it's time we ask ourselves:

- What parts of your living room cause you the most frustration and stress?
- Is it a room heavily neglected by the whole family? Maybe boundaries and cleaning times need to be implemented for everyone.
- Are there too many sentimental items adding to the clutter?
- Is your furniture awkwardly placed?
- Do you have exposed wires and cables amounting to visual clutter?
- Do you have sufficient storage options for your books, magazines, and DVDs?

### Recognize Challenges

One of the biggest challenges that those of us with ADHD face in our living rooms is not being able to differentiate between clutter in motion and clutter in stasis. Clutter in motion is a good type of mess. It consists of the items we take out of cabinets or drawers because we are using them. These items can make us feel comfortable and help us get things done. However, if we don't put these items back in their designated place, over time, they become clutter in stasis. Here, our ADHD brain stops recognizing them as a mess and decides to simply work around it. In simple terms, these are your doom piles. More often than not, the reason behind doom piles is that there is no designated home for the items. That's why I emphasize giving every belonging in your house a specific place.

### *Set Realistic Goals*

Who else wants more from their living room than a drop zone for neglected items? Personally, this room was my biggest motivator when it came to decluttering my house. My ultimate dream was to have my friends over for coffee and a clean place for me and my family to relax after a hard day. I know we all want to say goodbye to the sea of clutter and hello to a room that conveys calm. This leads me to ask, what is your living room goal? For some, comfort is a priority—fluffy blankets and big warm pillows on the couch. For others, the goal is an aesthetically pleasing room for family and friends to enjoy. Think about it and write it down because we are going to accomplish it!

## CLEAR THE PATH

*Declutter*

Adopting a systematic approach is going to help us get through this chaos a lot easier. Let's break this down into simple steps:

1. **Obvious clutter:** Grab a trash bag and start throwing out soda cans, magazines, tissues, and random take-out menus.
2. **Baskets and storage containers:** Any box or basket that you've accumulated items in during past cleaning sessions now deserves to be given a home or thrown away.
3. **Raggedy blankets:** A blanket will forever do its purpose of keeping you warm and cozy, but do you really need to keep that one that's fraying and has food stains all over it? Throw it out.
4. **Pillows:** If you own a pet and have had your couch pillows for multiple years, then consider taking a sniff of them and see if they're contributing to any foul odors in your house.
5. **Electronics:** If you have any outdated DVD players or consoles, then it's time to part ways. You might even be able to make some spare cash from them. Additionally, invest in a wire box behind your TV. You'll thank me when it comes to dusting and vacuuming.
6. **Toys:** Lego pieces, dolls, and action figures are all items that belong in a playroom or bedroom.

Just like that, you've decluttered your living room!

### Reading Material

While it's convenient for the whole family to leave things where they last used them, it can create a negative atmosphere as well as an undesired pattern of behavior. Every item requires a well-arranged space, starting with books and magazines. If you enjoy the latest celebrity gossip and flipping through a magazine in the evening with a nice glass of wine, then a magazine rack is the solution for you. Magazine racks are a cute and compact way to store all your articles; usually, they are the ideal size to slip right next to your sofa. However, if you're fond of delving into a novel while cozying up on your couch, then you really can't go wrong with a bookshelf. A bookshelf can also be used to store decorative trinkets, vases, and fake plants. It's a two-for-one deal.

### Minimalism Mindset

Have you ever considered that maybe you have too much furniture in your living room? Baskets, trunks, and cabinets are amazing at holding storage, but sometimes, we can abuse their power. We have the tendency to throw heaps of rubbish and clutter into them since no one can see them. They hide all our secrets for the cost of our living room space. Overcrowding our living room significantly impacts how we feel in it. Compact and cramped spaces leave us feeling restricted. Remove the items from each section of furniture and ask yourself if you've used it in the last year. If you haven't, then you probably don't care for it, and it should be donated or thrown out. If you have used the item, then find it a better home than your living room. Creating an open space will improve functionality, atmosphere, and cleanliness.

## STORAGE SOLUTIONS

### Shelves and Cabinets

We spend a lot of time in our living room with our families; hence, we must make our storage solutions meaningful and practical. Opting for built-in cabinets or free-standing shelves is one way to take full advantage of limited space. Built-in cabinets are perfect for those awkward spaces that never really had a purpose. If you need more space for your tables and seating arrangements, then consider a shelving system that is tall rather than broad. You can also accent shelving areas or built-in cabinets by adding a few coats of paint and some artistic décor. Moreover, swap out clean containers for wicker baskets; they offer the same level of organization while adding warmth and detail to your living area.

### Remote Control

Losing the remote control must be one of the most frustrating things in life. I may be exaggerating a little, but we really do need to find safe spaces to store these items. The traditional location for the controller is the coffee table; if you don't have one, add a Velcro strip to the back of the remote and to the side of the TV or bookshelf. This way, you'll have a designated space for the controller, and it's super creative! Alternatively, you could exchange decorative pieces with a tray or cute box to store a variety of electronics and remotes.

## CREATE ZONES

Throughout the following week, keep a notepad and pen handy in your living room. You will need to take notes on different zones where you and your family complete activities like watching TV, reading, and conversing. Sectioning your rooms and living spaces into zones will allow you to understand the best places to store your belongings. For instance, if you notice that you enjoy reading near the window, then it would be logical for you to organize books and bookshelves within that area. This will allow for maximum efficiency and practicality.

### Arrange Furniture

A house is not a home when furniture is randomly placed, lacking all functionality and purpose. Creating a flow within our living areas promotes balance and a sense of order and peace—a true necessity for a happy house.

The first step in any room is identifying a focal point, like a window, fireplace, or TV. This visually interesting feature will serve as the anchor we build around. Next, position the main furniture, like sofas and armchairs, to face and highlight the focal point. Make sure sightlines are unobstructed. Then, fill in functional pieces like side tables, lamps, and ottomans to complete the layout.

As you arrange furnishings, keep these do's and don'ts in mind:

Do

- orient furniture to enhance natural light
- incorporate built-in storage like bookcases
- add personal art and accents

Don't

- block doorways or walkways
- place the TV opposite a window
- overcrowd the space

By starting with a focal point and intentional furniture placement, you can create peaceful and practical living areas.

### Foster Interaction and Relaxation

If you're hoping for more social interaction from your family and less TV time, then moving around your sofas could make your dream come true. If you have a large living room, try placing two sofas opposite each other in the middle, breaking the distance with a coffee table. Make sure they're no bigger than 8 feet apart. However, if your living room isn't big enough for this, you can create a semi-circle by adding two chairs at either end of your sofa at a reasonable distance. Both seating arrangements promote conversation and are bound to revolutionize your living space.

## MANAGE DIGITAL DISTRACTIONS

For those of us who have little ones, we know that phones, video games, and DVDs are digital vortexes that hold our kid's attention captive. By organizing these devices correctly and keeping them out of sight, we might just be able to steal back a little more of their time. Implement the idiom "out of sight, out of mind." Avoid placing TVs and computers in your child's bedroom and instead choose a communal area like the living room. We can keep Xboxes and Switches in cabinets, as well as remote controls. This way, your child won't enter the living room and immediately turn on the TV or gaming console.

Media guidelines are paramount for little ones, not only so they complete their homework but also to keep them safe from online predators and overstimulating videos. After getting home from school, there could be a no-technology rule. Encourage conversation, working on homework, or reading a book; all things that can be done in the comfort of your living room. On weekends, suggest spending time in nature, such as going on hikes and walks or visiting museums and theaters. For those of us who have sneaky kids, ensure you have passwords and parental control enabled on laptops and iPads. When your child is allowed time on their device, it's paramount that it does not interfere with their sleeping schedule. We can facilitate this by ensuring our child has at least one hour before bed that is technology-free and allows time for winding down.

## PERSONALIZE YOUR SPACE

### *Create a Meaningful Atmosphere*

Placing photos of you with your family and loved ones is one of the easiest and quickest ways to make a house feel like a home. They don't require construction or nails; simply use a command strip. While painting walls can feel like a big task, a fresh coat of paint often symbolizes new beginnings and can be a super fun family project. However, if you don't feel like opening the tin of paint, consider some funky wallpaper designs. Maybe drop into the local art school and see what bargain art pieces are available to spice up your living room.

We often find joy in the little things, and we can easily implement them in our homes to create a warm and inviting atmosphere. For instance, flowers; getting in the habit of buying a fresh bouquet twice a month will brighten up any room, and they smell fantastic! Also, I can't be the only one who loves the feeling of a fluffy rug. Consider rolling one out and inviting warmth into your living space. Little personal touches from things that make you happy create a lovely and inviting home.

### *Less is More*

Balance is key when it comes to decorating our homes. We must keep our ADHD symptoms in mind, especially when decorations involve busy patterns that can lead to overstimulation or the inability to focus. Furthermore, we must decorate in moderation to not give the appearance of clutter. We have come so far on this journey; the last thing we want is a wall full of family photos looking dusty and causing headaches.

We all have a place in our hearts for beautiful and aesthetically pleasing homes. However, if we don't incorporate functionality into aesthetics, we will end up back at square one, having to declutter. When attempting to combine both everyday items and aesthetically pleasing ones, focus on symmetry. For example, open storage should have groups of threes or fives for items like books, as it is more pleasing to the eye. Incorporate your personal style and keep it simple.

You harnessed your hyper-focus to think outside the box with decorations and organizing. Implementing these strategies has allowed you and your family to enjoy time in a clean and orderly environment that emits warmth and peace. Now, get ready to clear the navigational system of your home, the hallway.

# LIVING ROOM CHECKLIST

This checklist is NOT meant to be completed in one day. Success comes through small consistent actions and not through big burnout sessions.

**Helpful tips:**

- STAY IN THE LIVING ROOM: Do not leave to re-home something until the room is complete.
- Listen to music, books, or podcasts to make it fun.
- Adopt the minimalist mindset: be serious about getting rid of things that no longer serve you.

Identify pain points:
_____
_____

Set Realistic Goals:
_____
_____

Plan how you will overcome distraction and stay on task:
_____
_____

☐ Make sure you have your three boxes labeled *Re-home, Trash, and Donate.*

☐ Declutter: pick up any misplaced items that don't belong in this room. This could be clothes, food, dishes, toys, mail, shoes, etc. Sort these items into the labeled boxes.

☐ Tables: clear off any coffee or end tables and give them a wipe down. As you place things back on tables, be honest about what purpose these items have. If the items take up so much space that the table cannot serve its purpose, then it's time to donate some things.

☐ Electronics: wipe down your TV screen and designate a place for the remote to live so you never lose it. Always put it back in this new home. Use wire boxes or ties to maintain a neat space.

☐ Couches: check under and between couch cushions for any lost items or food. Vacuum and wipe down the couches and chairs. Move any furniture around if you plan to re-arrange the room for a better flow

☐ Shelves: remove all decor, books, CDs, DVDs, baskets, etc. Wipe down the shelves and designate space for different categories. As you place items back on shelves, ask yourself how long it has been since you used each item. You do not need to hold onto DVDs you'll never watch again, or books you'll never read.

☐ Decor: your living space should reflect your personal style and energy. The decorations you choose should inspire you, but too many decorations will have the opposite effect. Keep it simple and pick your favorites.

☐ Plan a specific time each week to clean and tidy the living room to maintain the clutter-free environment: Day of week: _____ Time:_____

☐ Disperse the three boxes: throw away trash, drop-off donations, and re-home the items that did not belong in the living room.

# 10

# HALLWAYS AND CLOSETS

 *Figure out what you care about and let it motivate you.*

— JONATHAN MOONEY

These are the words of a man who couldn't read until the age of 12 due to dyslexia. Jonathan Mooney thrives off passion, stating that there's no magic pill, nor is there a big secret to success. The key is simply to find something that enthralls your entire body with love and inspiration and allow yourself to be driven by it from head to toe. In Mooney's early years of college, he tapped into a level of anger he had never experienced before. When enquiring about English literature classes, excited to follow his burning passion, he was judged, belittled, and told the courses were too intellectual for him. Jonathan had two options: either absorb the criticism and let it eat away at his self-esteem or harness the anger into positive actions. Graduating years later with an honors degree in literature, he was glad he chose the latter. The next time you come across a situation that frustrates, angers, or pains you, recall this story. Life presents us with copious amounts of situations in which we can grow and learn or hide and hurt. Ultimately, the decision is yours. I know which one I'd choose, don't you?

## ASSESS YOUR HALLWAYS AND CLOSETS

### *Identify Pain Points*

After a long, tiring day, the thought of going home and relaxing brings peace to my mind. However, I'm often rudely awakened by the mess at my front door, reminding me that my home is an utter disaster. If I'm lucky, I'll remember to avoid tripping over multiple pairs of shoes on my way to the bathroom. The thought of a nice, hot, steamy shower seems to relieve the stress of my chaotic home. But that never seems to last long, as my storage cabinet containing all my sheets and towels is just as big of a mess.

Entryways are the spaces that welcome us into our home; stepping inside should feel like a big warm embrace, not a cold remembrance of all the chores you have yet to complete. Our hallways are portals that transport us from one room to another, yet we feel cramped and stressed by the clutter when walking through them. The storage room should be easily accessible and tidy, but in my house, multiple items fall on me each time I open the door. These are the typical frustrations of my hallways and storage closet; what are yours?

- Do you have shoes scattered in front of the door?
- Are there coats and jackets stacked in messy piles waiting to be hung up?
- Are there sufficient hooks, cupboards, and cabinets for your necessities?
- Do you have a designated place for keys and mail?
- Have you neglected decorations, leaving the last season's up?
- Is there clutter occupying the floors?

*Recognize Challenges*

When it comes to entryways, I often find that we have the tendency to completely misuse built-in organization like hooks and shelves. We accidentally store every coat and jacket we own on three hooks while a sea of disorganized shoes roams freely on the floor. The same issue presents itself in our storage closets, an overbearing mess that lacks organization. This can be attributed to not implementing goals for this space. We disregard their importance because of how small they are and lack a vision for what we need and want within these areas. Additionally, we bring things in from work and casually dump the items by the door, forgetting they exist. In turn, they become clutter in stasis, meaning our ADHD brains will simply work around them and see them as a part of our hallways. But with intention and forethought, we can transform these small spaces into functional, organized areas that support our needs.

## *Set Realistic Goals*

Now, it's time to create a vision for how you want your hallway to function. What is the goal for your hallway? Your goals for your hallway can range from wanting a simple and sweet area that is perfect for welcoming guests to an area that reflects your personality through unique artwork and decor. What about your goals for your storage closet? Do you want an optimal organization that involves color-coded bins and labels? Are you simply aiming to avoid over-cramming time and time again? Ensure your goals are written down and detailed so our path to success is clear.

## CLEAR THE PATH

Creating clear and clean pathways allows us to make our way out the door without tripping over random knick-knacks or mountains of shoes. Let's approach the decluttering in sections, starting with what's visible outside any closet doors. Begin by removing items from hooks, shelves, and bins and sorting them into boxes of "keep," "donate," and "trash."

Once we have cleared space in our hallway, we can move on to the mess that hides behind closet doors. If we come across keepsakes and memorable items that we're going to find diffi-cult to part with, allocate a separate box for these and organize them at a later time. We need to limit the number of random items we have in our hallway and storage closets. We want to create a clean space to store jackets and coats rather than old lunch boxes, a random soccer ball, or shoes we'll never wear

CHAOS TO CALM | 133

again. For items like backpacks, umbrellas, hats, and scarves, we can use clear organizational bins to store them correctly. Remember to label every box for easy access.

### Sort and Categorize

Organizing your hallway closet by category allows for quick, efficient access to needed items. Group together seasonally used items—like hats, gloves, and umbrellas for cold weather or sunscreen and caps for warm weather. Keep pet supplies like leashes, collars, and toys in one bin. Have lighting essentials like bulbs, flashlights, and candles in another area. Other household closets may contain extra linen, cleaning supplies, or tools. Sort each closet according to its function. The key is designating a specific spot for certain items to live. Organizing your closet by category will allow you to grab what you need from one designated bin or area without rummaging to find everything you need just to walk the dog or light up the house during a power outage. With intentional categorization, you'll gain control of your closet chaos.

### Minimize Bulk

Unnecessary items are huge contributors to closet chaos; let's determine what we need to say goodbye to. Do you have a surplus of cleaning products? Vacuuming, sweeping, and mopping are essential on our journey to having a clean home, although if you're more inclined to pick up a broom than you are a vacuum, it's time to consider donating or selling. This rule can be applied to most items that are big, bulky, and consuming your closet space, such as exercise equipment or luggage you never use.

## STORAGE SOLUTIONS

Shelves are a super versatile method of storage; whether it's an awkward space under your stairs, at the front of your entryway, or in your closet, a shelf will fit no matter the size. They also act as transition zones when placed by your door, perfect for setting up a lovely-smelling diffuser and a tray to place your keys. Hooks are perfect for those of us who are often in a rush or have kids who always forget their coats on the way to school. A hook can be used as a visual reminder of what you need that day. They require a bit more maintenance as they are on display; nonetheless, they're an optimal use of storage. However, if you're looking for an alternative method that doesn't involve a screwdriver, go back to the basics and stick with baskets. Baskets offer a wide variety of styles, from clear containers that are stackable to trendy wicker or cotton bins. Bins, baskets, and containers are classics that'll never disappoint, especially in terms of those items you need to grab while walking out the door.

### Assess the Layout

Assessing the hallway involves considering dimensions and implementing objectives. For instance, one objective could be maintaining a hallway that is clear of overcrowded items. To obtain this objective, we must find storage solutions to maximize our space. Another objective could be finding somewhere to store shoes. From big spaces to small spaces, every house requires a home for its shoes. Fortunately, shoe cabinets are sleek and effortless, meaning they will fit practically anywhere near your door, and you can finally say goodbye to your sweaty gym trainers on the floor stinking up the house. Placing a storage ottoman or even a little stool next to it will provide a place to sit when removing our shoes. If you're limited to space in your entryway, swap out hooks for a rail in your hallway closet. This will save you space and allow your jackets to be easily accessible when in a rush.

### Labeling System

It's clear that labeling is the way of the future. You have adopted the labeling system and implemented it in various rooms in your house. To maintain the same level of consistency and clarity throughout your home, it's crucial you don't forget to label your storage bins in the storage closet. It is the perfect time to implement all the organizational hacks you've learned. With a sticky label and bright pen, you'll provide an extra touch of efficiency and tidiness to your closet. Now, you and your family will be able to find all the items you need when you need them.

### Enhance Safety and Mobility

Our hallways are high-traffic zones for our family and visitors, and we are usually in a rush to get places. This means we need efficient lighting to enhance visibility. Try opting for a bright ceiling fixture that provides an illuminated path within our hallways. Additionally, we need to be consistent with regular cleaning routines and positive habits. We don't want to revert back to inconsistency because it will lead to overcrowded hallways and tripping hazards.

## MAINTAIN THE PATH

*Implement a Weekly Routine*

Regular cleaning routines will allow us to maintain a beautifully kept house and improve hygiene. Our hallway cleaning routine should take place once a week and take no longer than thirty minutes, so set a timer. Begin by ensuring everything is in its designated home, allowing us to move on to wiping down surfaces with a microfiber cloth. Don't forget to disinfect door handles; they are a playground for nasty bacteria and sweat. Next, vacuum or sweep the floor, followed by a mop. Now, we should have a sparkling, clean hallway.

*Maintenance Habits*

Habits play a significant role in keeping an organized home. However, actions take time and consistency to become habits, so start small and aim big. Your first hallway habit involves daily maintenance, which means after all your kiddos, roommates, or family have come home, make sure to give the hallway one last look for unorganized shoes, coats, and belongings. If you find anything out of place, put it back where it belongs. Children can also be involved in this activity by using a star chart and rewards. Set a timer for the children to race toward the hallway and clean up their clutter; the child who finishes first earns a star on the chart. The child with the most stars earns a candy or five minutes of extra iPad time at the end of the week.

### Control the Flow

Items like mail, keys, and even parcels or Amazon delivery have a constant flow within most households. We must make a conscious decision not to randomly plop these items down in an organized mess; instead, we need to create a designated home for them. For example, place a small basket or bin in your entryway for your wallet and keys and another for your mail. Make it a habit to sort through your mail daily so important letters never go unnoticed, and junk mail never piles up. Mail and parcels are meant to be clutter in motion, not stationary clutter. Once they enter the house, disperse them to their proper place. Don't let them take root and grow into another doom pile.

### Embrace Simplicity

Minimalism embraces intentional living; this means that every-thing we own has a purpose. It is based around simplicity, aiming to reduce stress and anxiety by limiting clutter and our belongings. This often suggests that we need to throw out items that no longer bring us joy. You can try this by holding an item and asking the question, "Do you make me happy?" If you hesi-tate to answer, then opt for donating or throwing it away.

Moreover, minimalism focuses on incorporating neutral colors and natural material; this frees up our cognitive space, allowing us more room for gratitude and self-discovery.

By incorporating simple changes within your entryway, hallways, and closets, you have enabled free movement and ease within your home. You will no longer be met by clutter at your door but feel a warm embrace from a beautiful home that you have created. Our path has now taken us through every room in the house, but our journey is not yet finished. We have learned how to organize; now, we need to learn how to avoid its undoing. The key to consistency lies in the following chapter.

# HALLWAYS/CLOSETS CHECKLIST

This checklist is NOT meant to be completed in one day. Success comes through small consistent actions and not through big burnout sessions.

**Helpful tips:**

- Listen to music, books, or podcasts to make it fun.
- Adopt the minimalist mindset: be serious about getting rid of things that no longer serve you.

Identify pain points:
_____
_____

Set Realistic Goals:
_____
_____

Plan how you will overcome distraction and stay on task:
_____
_____

☐ Make sure you have your three boxes labeled *Re-home, Trash, and Donate.*

☐ Floor: clear any obvious clutter and sort into the labeled boxes.

**\*With the floor and benches clear, now is a good time to disperse the items we've sorted through and keep the hallway clear before continuing.**

☐ Shelves/cabinets: go through any shelves or cabinets one at a time and sort items. Wipe down the shelves or cabinets. Return only the items that serve their purpose within the hallway. Designate a basket or tray for everyday items like car keys, wallets, and mail.

☐ Coat racks/hooks: go through all of the coats and sweatshirts on these hooks and be prepared to donate the ones you no longer wear or have a need for. Make sure to store off-season items in a different location to rotate as the seasons change.

☐ Closets: assign each closet within the home a specific storage function. For example, the entryway closet can home dog leashes, umbrellas, flashlights, and boots. The closet nearest the bedrooms can home extra linens. Another closet can home your cleaning supplies.

☐ Go through the closets one at a time. Sort out any items that no longer serve their purpose, and any items that will function better in a different closet. Dust and wipe down. Return items that belong, categorizing them based on function and accessibility.

☐ Plan a specific time each week to clean and tidy the hallways to maintain the clutter-free environment: Day of week:_____ Time:_____

☐ Disperse the three boxes: throw away trash, drop-off donations, and re-home the items that did not belong in the hallways and closets.

# 11

# MAKING IT STICK

 *Cleaning and organizing is a practice, not a project.*

— MEAGAN FRANCIS

When I first embarked on my own journey of organization, I quite literally wanted to rip my hair out. I was putting all my energy into deep cleaning, and two days later, my house would be a complete mess once again. It was exhausting, coming home from work stressed and somehow mustering up the motivation to wipe, dust, and vacuum every corner, yet it was never enough. If someone had said to me cleaning is a practice and not a project, I would have laughed. What is there to practice about cleaning? It's just wiping a few counters and taking out the trash, right?

Wrong! I was so so wrong! Cleaning is so much more than just a few simple sprays of disinfectant or a sweep here and there. It encompasses layers of organization, positive reinforcement, and transformative habits. To establish an organized and clean home, I had to shift my cognitive state and make mental clarity a priority. I needed to spend days, weeks, and months building myself up with compassion and self-love. I had to embrace my ADHD symptoms and accept my unorganized self for who I was. Accepting the past was the only way for me to move forward and revolutionize my life. Once my emotional journey had led me to this point, I decided to forget everything I thought I knew about cleaning and start from zero. Day by day, one step at a time, I practiced the art of organization, purging all my belongings and keeping what brought me joy. I began practicing labeling, color coding, and cleaning routines in my spare time, ultimately changing my life for the better.

If someone told me today that cleaning was a practice and not a project, I'd smile ear to ear, knowing the battles they have conquered. Embarking on this journey of discovery isn't one that is particularly easy, but it is worth it.

## FIND WHAT WORKS FOR YOU

Learning to clean the house with ADHD can be a challenge. That is why it's so important to find routines that work specifically for you. Think of neurodivergence as a Swiss army knife; many people will only see the blade, the ADHD. They will assume that just because of your diagnosis, cleaning and organizing are impossible tasks. However, much like a Swiss army knife, which has multiple tools for various tasks, the ADHD brain has a multitude of skill sets and abilities waiting to be demonstrated. The hardship is discovering how and when to utilize these incredible abilities.

A primary reminder should be that we don't always need to deep clean. Deep cleaning requires a multitude of hours as well as incredible amounts of energy, motivation, and determination. I know for me, it would be extremely difficult to not only find the time but also the desire to do that once a week or even a month. The idea is not to force something that doesn't work for you; if cleaning and organizing in small manageable chunks is what works for you, then stick to it.

Those of us with an ADHD brain will know that if we don't plan what we need to do and when we need to do it, that thing will most likely never get done. So, invest in a good planner; there are even organizers and diaries specifically tailored to those with ADHD.

Speaking of planning, create cleaning routines and rituals. Cleaning routines will save you on those busy days when you don't feel like cleaning. Instead of wandering around like a headless chicken, questioning what the next step is, you'll already have it on autopilot. Additionally, you'll know just how much time is required and be able to set a timer to keep you on track. Bear in mind that life has its funny moments that can interfere with schedules and planning, so don't get too tied up if you miss a day or two. Consistency lies in getting back on track once you've fallen off.

Start small and aim big. For many of us, cleaning and organizing is a whole new world that we are just discovering, so we do not want to jump all in. In the first few weeks, start small;

you can try the Five Things method in any room. For example, in the kitchen:

1. Put dirty dishes in the dishwasher.
2. Put all food away.
3. Wipe down the counters.
4. Sweep the floor.
5. Take out the trash.

You've broken down the primary issues in a kitchen into easy, manageable steps, subsiding that overwhelming feeling. Now that you've accomplished your first five tasks, you can aim big for the future. Write down cleaning goals such as "I will be able to consistently follow cleaning routines within the next six months."

Additionally, don't be afraid to reach out to your loved ones. Those who love you are going to be proud and inspired by the journey you are embarking on. There is no shame or guilt in needing an extra hand. Moreover, make sure to take care of yourself and prioritize healthy foods, as well as exercise. A clear mind creates a clear home.

## 10 TIPS FOR SUCCESS

1. **Plan:** create weekly plans of chores to stay on track.
2. **Time:** set alarms and timers to keep you on track and focused.
3. **Become an influencer:** influence your family and friends to join you on video calls when it is decluttering

time. You will motivate each other and increase enjoyment.

4. **Family cleaning schedule:** create a visible planner for your kids or partner to see. Allow them to help with placing things like toys and socks back in their designated areas.

5. **Buy less:** buying is the source of clutter. Suppress the urge to buy new things and save that money for a holiday.

6. **Categorize:** keep related items all in one spot to prevent you from running around the house all day.

7. **Have a place for everything and everything in its place:** if everything has a home, then there's no excuse for leaving things lying around.

8. **Avoid boredom:** if cleaning bores you, put some funky music on in the background or listen to an audiobook.

9. **Reward yourself:** treat yourself for staying consistent, especially when cleaning communal areas, as the mess might not even be yours.

10. **Stay positive:** even on days when you can't complete all the chores. Something is better than nothing.

## COMMIT TO THE LIFESTYLE

 *You do not rise to the level of your goals. You fall to the level of your systems.*

— JAMES CLEAR

He's right. The human brain is a survival mechanism designed to keep you safe and hasn't evolved even though humans have. The brain is made up of three responses that form the Motivational Triad—seek pleasure, avoid pain, and conserve energy. Your brain won't actively make a choice to create a system, form an energy-eating habit that develops into a ritual, or undertake uncomfortable tasks, as this translates as pain inside the brain. So, creating systems is something that may go against your very nature, but it is absolutely vital to being successful in anything you do. James Clear makes it easy using four principles, which we will discuss later on in this chapter. All these components work in harmony with your Motivational Triad, and from here on in, you can begin to take control of your mind, habits, goals, and dreams.

## OVERCOME PROCRASTINATION

Having an ADHD brain means that we are often in a world of procrastination. Common phrases entering our heads or leaving our mouths are "I'll do it tomorrow," "I work better under pressure," and even "I'll start once I'm in the right mood." Consequently, we begin to pay the price of our own actions or lack of action, having problems arise at work and even at home. Our bosses may be sick and tired of our never-ending list of excuses as to why we didn't complete our tasks, whereas our partners at home are disappointed in us for postponing our cleaning routines for the third week in a row. Now, our friends, family, and colleagues see us as lazy because they can't possibly understand our internal battle.

*Combat Perfectionism*

Once you have recognized your procrastination tendencies, you can begin to find solutions to break this bad habit. Your main focus is to break big tasks into small manageable chunks that are easy to understand and achieve. Smaller tasks make work and responsibilities feel less overwhelming. You can get a piece of paper or notebook and start dissecting all the things you need to do within your task. Then, you can arrange them by order or urgency, slowly ticking one of them at a time. Make sure to place the list of broken-down tasks in a visible area to keep track of how much you have left to complete. Don't forget that perfection is not a requirement. Imperfections allow us to learn and grow, so if you find yourself only able to complete half of a task, avoid negative thoughts and doubts; doing something is better than doing nothing.

## BUILD MOMENTUM AND MAINTAIN MOTIVATION

The best way to build up motivation is by doing something you enjoy. As we know, our ADHD brain is very selective as to what tasks it will motivate us for; thus, going for a coffee, meeting up with some friends, or partaking in your favorite hobby is a great start. Just make sure that this activity doesn't absorb your entire day, and set a timer on for half an hour to maintain productivity. Once your enjoyable activity time is over, start your project or task no matter how hard or poorly it turns out. The initial push to begin is always the toughest; that's why we must break through it. By doing a task directly after something that brings you happiness, you can condition your brain to associate the task with that positive feeling. Over time, this can help transform dreaded chores into more pleasant routines.

Moreover, your work environment must be suitable for your needs. Ignore the conventional tactics and think outside of the box. If listening to soft instrumental music doesn't improve your focus, try heavy metal or rap. The ADHD brain is super unique, so it just might work!

You can also build your own deadline goals. For instance, if you usually hand in projects on the deadline, make a personal goal to hand in the next project one day before the cut-off point. Not only will you impress your superiors, but you'll also feel empowered and proud of yourself.

### *Self-Assess, Adapt and Refine*

To be able to assess our behavior and actions, we have to understand key areas of our lives that are majorly influential. We must become aware of these five concepts:

1. **Emotions.** Having emotional intelligence means understanding what you feel, how this feeling influences your thoughts and actions, and the cause of this feeling. By understanding these three factors, we are better equipped to direct our emotions in a healthier way.
2. **Needs.** Being able to understand the needs that influence our behavior will, in turn, explain how they affect our relationships. Some examples of needs are affection, esteem, power, and control. When we are

denied these needs, it can leave us feeling angry and frustrated.

3. **Habits.** These are the behaviors we repeat continuously.
4. **Values.** These allow us to stay aligned with our priorities.
5. **Personality.** Understanding our personality will help us avoid entering situations that are high-stress; instead, we exchange them for situations we will enjoy.

These five aspects have a significant impact on our day-to-day experience. In terms of refining and adapting our personal system, we can begin by taking time to reflect on our strengths and weaknesses. Becoming aware of what we're good at and not so good at means we can finally use them to our benefit. For example, if we know that we're impeccable with numbers but struggle with words, when we come across a word problem, we already know the solution is to talk to a colleague who can help.

Additionally, we can improve our intuitive decision-making skills, also known as the "gut feeling." If we learn to adapt and understand our emotions, essentially becoming more emotionally intelligent, we can start to make superior decisions by trusting our feelings when our head isn't making any sense.

Moreover, understanding what makes us angry or frustrated can assist us in eradicating negative self-talk. Start by identifying your trigger; for example, if you experience anger because you're not progressing at work or at home, perhaps the underlying trigger is a fear of failure. Once you understand the cause of the anger, you can begin to eliminate thoughts such as "I'm useless and will never complete this task" and replace them with positivity, "I understand this task is difficult, but I know I am capable, smart, and have the ability to succeed." The key is to be aware when these thoughts arise in our brain as well as adapt an empathetic attitude toward ourselves.

## PRINCIPLES FOR SUCCESS

As we reach the end of this book, it's vital that we create systems to ensure our new habits and strategies last us a lifetime. One of the best ways to do this is by following James Clear's Atomic Habits technique. Previously, we learned that James utilizes four principles. These principles allow us to not only create life-long habits but also eliminate negative ones. The principles are:

1. **Make it obvious:** It really is as simple as it sounds; cleaning routines, to-do lists, and chores must be in plain sight. Place them in locations where your eyes are drawn to them, make them stand out, and ensure they are recognizable and clear. Visual reminders and cues emphasize consistency and allow us to understand what our next step is. Additionally, it's crucial we implement our labeling and color-coding systems to facilitate this process. If we know where everything goes, then we are one step closer to organization.
2. **Make it attractive:** No one said cleaning had to be boring. Enhance the time you spend cleaning by playing some music in the background or even listening to your

favorite podcast. Plus, if you're like me and love aesthetically pleasing items, invest in those cute storage bins or that bright pink vacuum. Incorporate the little things that bring you joy into cleaning, and you might even have fun!

3. **Make it easy:** Break down every task into small manageable chunks. Our ADHD brain can leave us jumping into tasks without an end goal in sight or even procrastinating for months on end because we're too overwhelmed. We have made the decision to break this cycle and strive for success, so we must create strategic plans when tackling big tasks. Additionally, keep it simple. We don't need six different cleaning supplies for different surfaces, and we don't need to micro-organize every nook and cranny of our house.

4. **Make it satisfying:** Reward yourself! Embarking on this journey was not an easy step to take, and neither is decluttering your entire house and revolutionizing your habits. Set milestones for achieving your goals and reward yourself once you've accomplished them. You can even invite your family along with you to celebrate your new life.

I can guarantee that these four principles will set you up for success. By simply implementing each one, you will become closer and closer to a lifetime of mental clarity and relaxation. You will be creating a house that not only you but your whole family can proudly call their home—taking back control from the chaos and revealing the ultimate power of a calm way of living.

*Fail Upwards*

We all know that creating lifelong habits starts with small achievable goals and building on them. Slowly, we create routines and new behaviors, but how do we maintain this? Well, you'll need to stay consistent, even on the day you don't feel like it. It will require patience and embracing not only your ADHD symptoms but also the journey to the fullest. Self-compassion will come in handy for days when you fall off track, but remember to replace negative doubts with positive action. Longevity will arise from the moments you thought were deal breakers. Ultimately, share your success and let your loved ones feel proud of the person you're becoming. Small failures are inevitable, but they do not mean defeat. The only true failure is giving up entirely. When you stumble, simply dust yourself off, adjust, and get back on track. With time, you'll discover what works for you and be able to maintain consistency.

## Light the Way for Others

The thought that you are now developing daily habits, identifying pain points, and clearing the clutter from a myriad of rooms in your home fills me with inspiration. I know how overwhelming clutter can be, but the magic begins by simply starting—one room at a time, one small goal at a time. And guess what? You have the chance to pass on the many handy tips contained in these pages.

Simply by sharing your honest opinion of this book and a little about your own journey, you'll show new readers where they can find all the information they need to come home to clean, tidy, beautifully organized spaces.

**TAKE A MOMENT TO SHARE YOUR THOUGHTS!**

Thank you so much for your support. I can't tell you how much difference it makes.

# Scan the QR code here

# CONCLUSION

As we reach the end of this book, preparing ourselves to bid farewell, remember this is not the end of your journey, but just the beginning. We navigated our way through tremendous complexities, delving deep into the fascinating realm of our ADHD minds—not just understanding but immersing ourselves in profound knowledge of the cognitive and psycho- logical aspects of ADHD. We are now equipped with fierce tools to navigate our symptoms, crafting success from emotional dysregulation and working memory deficits. You have the power to turn a perceived weakness into a fountain of strength. The journey started to unfold, kicking off with kitchen chaos. You embraced the difficulties and harnessed the transformative potential in the heart of your home, creating an organized and functional space. We progressed from one room to another, decluttering every inch to reveal a plain canvas ready for your new life. You cleared away the fog with revolu- tionary storage techniques, allowing for clarity and calm. You have adopted goal-setting techniques that will nurture a life full of accomplishments and victories. Hearing stories from Ty Pennington to Adam Levine demonstrated that we are never truly alone on this path.

Enjoy your sanctuary of serenity and feel proud of what you have accomplished. Your home is now an organized paradise ready for any situation. Invite your friends over, tell your neighbors, and call your family; you deserve the praise.

Your journey continues to unfold. Implement your newly gained knowledge and use valuable strategies, as well as practical tips. Execute your empowering techniques to boost productivity and eliminate clutter. Harness your hyper-focus and expect to create lifelong habits that empower your ADHD mindset. Bear in mind that there will be days where you stray from the path; whether you're sick, too busy, or simply just too tired, it is okay. See your mistakes as stepping stones, ones that will bring you closer to new insight and self-compassion.

Utilize this book as inspiration that will guide you through a path of discovery. Unfortunately, I can't provide a solution to everyone's unique ADHD symptoms or individual living situation. However, what I can offer you is a toolkit, one that has copious amounts of strategies and techniques to make your life far easier. I encourage you to read the introductory stories in moments where ADHD makes you feel isolated. I know how it feels and want to assure you that you are never alone; there are tons of online communities and forums waiting to hear your voice and opinions. Get out there and share your story; you might just feel a little less lonely.

I want to express my gratitude and admiration for every reader; thank you for embarking on this journey with me. I hope this book not only serves as a guide to transform your house into a serene living environment but also an enlightened path to a new way of living, one that will improve every aspect of your world. Taking the first step to transforming your life can be exceptionally challenging. Deciding to make revolutionary changes often means stepping into the unknown, encompassing you with anxiety and uncertainty. Fear of failure was always my biggest struggle, usually paralyzing me from stepping outside of my comfort zone. However, you acted with bravery and fearlessness, prepared to face any challenge. As you move forward, I urge you to be gentle with yourself; setbacks are normal. Have patience and love, and always embrace your ADHD. After all, it's a unique asset to have!

Your feedback matters. I would love to hear the opinions of brilliant ADHD minds. If you would like to leave a message or even a review, I would greatly appreciate it. Once again, thank you for trusting me with your time and dedication. May this book be used as a source of inspiration and light, especially in moments when you need it most.

# REFERENCES

Acostello. (2010, April 1). *Creative ways to color-code your home.* https://www. alejandra.tv/blog/2010/04/creative-ways-to-color-code-your-home

ADDitude Editor. "10 ADHD Quotes to Save for a Bad Day." ADDitude. January 14, 2020. https://www.additudemag.com/slideshows/adhd-quotes-for-a-bad-day/

*Adam Levine Talks About ADHD.* (n.d.). Casa pacifica centers for children and families. https://www.casapacifica.org/news/blog/ adam_levine_talks_about_adhd/

Amanda Garrity. (2020, January 30). *40 creative bathroom storage ideas to make the most of a small layout.* https://www.goodhousekeeping.com/home/orga nizing/tips/g810/small-bathroom-storage/

*Autonomous.* (2018, November 2). https://www.autonomous.ai/ourblog/16-ways-to-organize-office-desk

Avis-Riordan, K. (2018, March 17). *The big declutter challenge: How to create a clutter-free, clean and organised living room.* House Beautiful. https://www. housebeautiful.com/uk/lifestyle/storage/a19442463/how-to-declutter-living-room-storage-ideas/

Babington-Stitt, T. K. (2022, June 1). *35 Living room storage ideas to curb the clutter and restore the calm.* Ideal Home. https://www.idealhome.co.uk/ living-room/living-room-ideas/living-room-storage-ideas-to-restore-order-to-your-space-87798

Barbour, H. (2020, June 16). *Famous people with ADHD [100+ Actors, Entrepre-neurs, Athletes, Musicians & More!].* Ongig Blog. https://blog.ongig.com/ diversity-and-inclusion/famous-people-with-adhd/

Barkley, R., & Ph.D. (2021, September 20). *DESR: Why deficient emotional self-regulation is central to ADHD (and Largely Overlooked).* ADDitude. https:// www.additudemag.com/desr-adhd-emotional-regulation/

Becker, Joshua. (n.d.). *Decluttering your kitchen & reclaiming your home's heart.* https://www.becomingminimalist.com/how-to-declutter-your-kitchen/

Blain, T. (2022, October 20). *Habit stacking for ADHD.* Verywell Mind. https:// www.verywellmind.com/habit-stacking-definition-steps-benefits-for-adhd-6751145

Blasdel, B. (2023, February 8). *The best ADHD-friendly hacks for staying organized. vice.* https://www.vice.com/en/article/m7g8b3/adhd-organization-products-hacks

*Calming ADHD Bedroom Ideas: creating a soothing sleeping environment.* (2023, May 12). Sleepout. https://sleepoutcurtains.com/blogs/home/calming-adhd-bedroom-ideas

CDC. (2022, August 9). *What is ADHD?* Centers for disease control and prevention. https://www.cdc.gov/ncbddd/adhd/facts.html

CHADD. (2018a). *Myths and misunderstandings - CHADD.* CHADD. https://chadd.org/about-adhd/myths-and-misunderstandings/

CHADD. (2018b). *Psychosocial treatments - CHADD.* CHADD. https://chadd.org/for-parents/psychosocial-treatments/

CIH Admin. (2022, April 18). *Interior design: How to achieve "flow" in your home.* https://cihdesign.com/interior-design-how-to-achieve-flow-in-your-home/

Cleveland Clinic. (2017). *Attention deficit disorder (ADHD).* Cleveland Clinic. https://my.clevelandclinic.org/health/diseases/4784-attention-deficithyperactivity-disorder-adhd

Cleveland Clinic. (2022, June 5). *Executive dysfunction: What it is, symptoms & treatment.* Cleveland Clinic. https://my.clevelandclinic.org/health/symptoms/23224-executive-dysfunction

Cleveland Clinic. (2022, July 7). *Cerebellum: What it is, function & anatomy.* Cleveland Clinic.https://my.clevelandclinic.org/health/body/23418-cerebellum#:~:text=Your%20cerebellum%20is%20a%20part

ClutterFreeAdmin987123. (2023, February 14). *15 ADHD Kitchen organizing tips that really work.* The Simple Daisy. https://thesimpledaisy.com/15-adhd-kitchen-organizing-tips-that-really-work/

*Colour Coding Items & Utensils | How to colour code in kitchens.* (2013). Nisbets Articles. Nisbets.co.uk; Nisbets. https://www.nisbets.co.uk/colourcodingitems

Combiths, S. (2021, October 14). *21 Ideas for keeping a perpetually clean kitchen.* The Kitchn. https://www.thekitchn.com/clean-kitchen-ideas-22967553

Combiths, S. (2021, November 10). *20 Sneaky ways to declutter your kitchen.* The Kitchn. https://www.thekitchn.com/sneaky-ways-to-declutter-kitchen-23088977

Corriveau, M. (2020, June 17). *7 Benefits of being organized in your home and life.*

Life with Less Mess. https://www.lifewithlessmess.com/benefits-of-being-organized/

CottageSoup. (2021, November 11). *Can you have adhd and be organized?* Reddit. https://www.reddit.com/r/ADHD/comments/qr88os/can_you_have_adhd_and_be_organized/?utm_source=share&utm_medium=web2x&context=3

Curatolo, P., D'Agati, E., & Moavero, R. (2010). The Neurobiological basis of ADHD. *Italian Journal of Pediatrics, 36*(1), 79. https://doi.org/10.1186/1824-7288-36-79

Darcy. (2020, January 14). *5 Simple tips to start a clean living lifestyle.* Preserving My Sanity. https://preservingmysanity.com/5-simple-tips-to-start-a-clean-living-lifestyle/

*David Neeleman.* (n.d.). Dyslexia help. http://dyslexiahelp.umich.edu/david-neeleman

Diamond, A., Ph.D., FRSC, FAPA, FAPS, & FSEP. (2022, February 24). *How to sharpen executive functions: Activities to hone brain skills.* ADDitude. https://www.additudemag.com/how-to-improve-executive-function-adhd/

Ditzell, J. (2022, May 18). *ADHD and emotions: Relationship and tips to manage.* Healthline. https://www.healthline.com/health/adhd/emotional-regulation#tips

Dodson, W. (2018, February 13). *ADHD & the interest-based nervous system.* ADDitude. https://www.additudemag.com/adhd-brain-chemistry-video/

Dowle, J. (2023, February 10). *9 Things a professional declutterer won't keep in their bedroom.* House Beautiful. https://www.housebeautiful.com/uk/lifestyle/storage/a40642342/how-to-declutter-bedroom/

Dupar, L. (2011, September 19). *Simple ADHD-friendly office organization tips.* HealthyPlace. https://www.healthyplace.com/blogs/livingwithadultadhd/2011/09/simple-office-organization-tips-for-people-with-adhd

Eaken, K. (2023, January 31). *A clean and organized home has many benefits.* Cleanheartmaids. https://cleanheartmaids.com/clean-and-organized-home/

Editors, Add. (2013, June 17). *How to form good habits with adult ADHD.* ADDitude. https://www.additudemag.com/how-to-form-good-habits-with-adult-adhd/

Editors, Add. (2016a, November 28). *10 ADHD quotes to save for a bad day.* ADDitude. https://www.additudemag.com/slideshows/adhd-quotes-for-a-bad-day/

Editors, Add. (2016b, November 28). *13 Clutter hacks for the easily overwhelmed.* ADDitude. https://www.additudemag.com/slideshows/quick-cleaning-tips-for-the-easily-overwhelmed/

Editors, Add. (2021, April 27). *Doing laundry with ADHD: 5 helpful tips.* Www.additudemag.com. https://www.additudemag.com/doing-laundry-tips-adhd/#:~:text=Set%20a%20timer%20on%20your

Editors, Add. (2022, April 13). *Kitchen organizing tips for cluttered adults with ADHD.* Www.additudemag.com. https://www.additudemag.com/slideshows/kitchen-organizing-tips-for-adhd/

Editors, O. (2023, January 2). *9 Best natural cleaning products for a nontoxic home.* The Good Trade. https://www.thegoodtrade.com/features/natural-eco-friendly-cleaning-products-for-the-conscious-home/

Eisenberg, R. (2021, July 22). *ADHD kitchen organization - tools and tips!.* The Practical Kitchen. https://thepracticalkitchen.com/adhd-kitchen-organization-tips-tools/

Emotional Dysregulation & ADHD. (n.d.). *Thriving with ADHD.* https://thrivingwithadhd.com.au/emotional-dysregulation/

Faraone, S. V., & Larsson, H. (2019). Genetics of attention deficit hyperactivity disorder. *Molecular Psychiatry, 24*(4), 562–575. https://doi.org/10.1038/s41380-018-0070-0

FastBraiin. (2021, June 29). *6 Easy tips for simplifying ADHD and house cleaning.* FastBraiin. https://www.fastbraiin.com/blogs/blog/adhd-and-house-cleaning

Fisher, D. (2019, November 3). *ADHD Couldn't stop me from climbing mount Everest.* https://www.additudemag.com/lofty-ambitions/

*5 tips for streamlining your laundry routine.* (2012, April 12). HowStuffWorks. https://home.howstuffworks.com/home-improvement/household-hints-tips/cleaning-organizing/5-tips-for-streamlining-your-laundry-routine.htm

Fountain, L. (2023, May 2). *Best material for bed sheets.* Sleep Foundation. https://www.sleepfoundation.org/best-sheets/best-material-for-bed-sheets

Gaskill, L. (2016, April 17). *10 Tips to streamline laundry day.* Houzz. https://www.houzz.com/magazine/10-tips-to-streamline-laundry-day-stsetivw-vs~64156639

Gaskill, L. (2022, June 19). *20 Ways to personalize a new house.* Houzz. https://www.houzz.com/magazine/20-ways-to-personalize-a-new-house-stse

tivw-vs~58406131

Godman, H. (2012, July 19). *ADHD Struggles: 8 Obstacles and how to overcome them*. Psych Central. https://psychcentral.com/adhd/adhd-struggles-coping-tips#recap

Godman, H. (2021, February 5). *Midlife ADHD? Coping strategies that can help*. Harvard Health. https://www.health.harvard.edu/blog/mid-life-adhd-coping-strategies-that-can-help-2021020521862

Hakim, H. (2021, June 29). *Cleaning with ADHD: Why is it so difficult? What can you do?* hyperlychee. https://hyperlychee.com/blogs/articles/cleaning_with_adhd

Hillger, V. (2016, October 20). *How to make your sock drawer amazing in 10 minutes or less*. simplify Experts. https://simplifyexperts.com/organize-sock-drawer-10-minutes-less/

*How to separate & sort your laundry like an expert*. (2023, March 17). The Laundress. https://www.thelaundress.com/blogs/tips/how-to-sort-laundry

*How to use a garage more effectively for holiday decoration storage*. (n.d.). Www.garageliving.com. https://www.garageliving.com/blog/garage-holiday-decoration-storage-tips

*Step-By-Step Guide to decluttering a garage: Garage declutter tips*. (2022, October 6). Simplify Create Inspire. Simplifycreateinspire. https://www.simplify createinspire.com/garage-declutter/

*Get started now*. (2023, February 17). The Spruce Eats.https://www.thes pruceeats.com/welcome-to-organization-week-5087036

Josel, L. (2021, June 1). *Q: "How can we slay our kids' messy bedroom this summer?"* ADDitude. https://www.additudemag.com/messy-bedroom-small-spaces-adhd/

Joyner, L. (2021, July 11). *7 Simple habits for a clean kitchen*. House Beautiful. https://www.housebeautiful.com/uk/lifestyle/cleaning/a36965751/clean-kitchen-habits/

kathleen.p.lamothe. (2021, June 28). *How I made putting away my laundry easier on my ADHD brain*. The P.E.R.M.A. Geek. https://thepermageek.com/adhd-laundry-solution/

Kerr, J. (2018, March 23). *5 Ugly truths your cluttered life reveals about you*. Organized Interiors Blog. https://www.organizedinteriors.com/blog/cluttered-life/#:~:text=A%20cause%20and%20effect%20of

Klein, A. (2021, June 24). *Tips on how to focus with ADHD*. Psych Central. https://psychcentral.com/adhd/adhd-tips-to-fire-up-your-focus#why-icant-focus

kristen. (2020, October 13). *Office organization and ADHD*. Sorted Out. https://www.sortedout.com/office-organizing-adhd-tips/

Lagustan, M. (2021, September 10). *A complete guide on personalizing your bedroom.* Crownaisia. https://www.crownasia.com.ph/news-and-blogs/lifestyle-blogs/selected/the-only-guide-youll-need-in-personalizing-your-bedroom

Larkin, E. (2022, December 9). *4 Smart ways to declutter your bedroom*. The Spruce. https://www.thespruce.com/cutting-clutter-in-your-bedroom-2647994

Lenner, M. (2021, October 14). *Types of ADHD: Inattentive, hyperactive-impulsive, and more*. Healthline. https://www.healthline.com/health/adhd/three-types-adhd#can-it-be-prevented

Levine, A. (2013, April 19). *Maroon 5's Adam Levine: "ADHD isn't a bad thing."* ADDitude. https://www.additudemag.com/adam-levine-adhd-is-not-a-bad-thing-and-you-are-not-alone/

Low, K. (2022, January 4). *Using your working memory with ADD as a therapeutic strategy*. Verywell Mind. https://www.verywellmind.com/add-and-work ing-memory-20796

Lyons, G. (2022, January 13). *What-is-cortisol*. Health Central. https://www. healthcentral.com/condition/cushings-syndrome/what-is-cortisol

Main, B. (2020 5). *Go paperless: Digital organization tips for adults with ADHD*. Www.additudemag.com. https://www.additudemag.com/paperless-digi tal-organization-adult-adhd-paperwork/

Mandel, H. (2011, April 6). *"I have a tough time being with myself.".* ADDitude; ADDitude. https://www.additudemag.com/howie-mandel-ocd/

Mariechristine. (2019, April 12). *Reclaiming space: Putting together the perfect garage*. Bestar. https://www.bestar.com/putting-together-the-perfect-garage/

Mendelsohn, H. (2023, January 13). *31 Bathroom storage ideas that are serious game changers*. House Beautiful. https://www.housebeautiful.com/life style/organizing-tips/g25138857/bathroom-storage-ideas/

Mom, T. (2023, June 12). *Digital addiction and ADHD: A toxic combination*. TechDetox Box. https://www.techdetoxbox.com/screen-time-problems/adhd/

Moon, A. (2023, May 2). *How to keep your room clean*. WikiHow. https://www. wikihow.com/Keep-Your-Room-Clean

Mooney, J. (2023, August 23). *Jonathan Mooney on goal setting and motivation in teens with LD or ADHD.* Great Schools.org. https://www.greatschools.org/gk/articles/goal-setting-motivation-teens-ld-or-ad-hd/

Morin, A. (n.d.). *8 Common myths about ADHD.* Www.understood.org. https://www.understood.org/en/articles/common-myths-about-adhd

Munir, DR. M. (2022, August 23). *ADHD hyperactive-impulsive type — Talkspace.* Mental Health Conditions. https://www.talkspace.com/mental-health/conditions/attention-deficit-hyperactivity-disorder/types/hyperactive-impulsive-adhd/

Nast, C. (2022, November 8). *20 Useful tips on decluttering and organizing your kitchen on a budget.* Architectural Digest India. https://www.architecturaldigest.in/story/20-useful-tips-on-decluttering-and-organizing-your-kitchen-on-a-budget/

NHS. (2021, December 24). *Causes - Attention deficit hyperactivity disorder (ADHD).* NHS. https://www.nhs.uk/conditions/attention-deficit-hyperactivity-disorder-adhd/causes/

Novotni, M. (2023, May 9). Stop ADHD Procrastination: Getting things done. Www.additudemag.com. https://www.additudemag.com/stop-adhd-procrastination/

Noyce, E. (2023, March 23). *Cleaning with ADHD: 7 Realistic tips for neurodivergent brains.* Www.getinflow.io. https://www.getinflow.io/post/cleaning-tips-for-adhd-adults

Pemberton, C. (2019, November 18). *Why can't I focus? 8 Reasons and solutions for the distracted brain.* Freedom Matters. https://freedom.to/blog/why-cant-i-focus-8-reasons-and-solutions-for-the-distracted-brain/

Philips, L. (2022, July 25). *10 Things in your living room you should toss right now.* Real Simple. https://www.realsimple.com/home-organizing/organizing/organizing-living-room/declutter-living-room

Poplin, J. (2022, February 3). *How to declutter your bathroom fast.* The Simplicity Habit. https://www.thesimplicityhabit.com/how-to-declutter-your-bathroom/

Posner, J. (2006, October 6). *9 ADHD myths and fallacies that perpetuate stigma.* ADDitude. https://www.additudemag.com/adhd-myths-and-facts-learn-the-truth-about-attention-deficit/

Premed101925. (2022, November 29). *Do you ever store something in a safe space so you won't lose it, and then you forget where the safe space is?* Reddit. https://

www.reddit.com/r/ADHD/comments/z89zf0/do_you_ever_store_something_in_a_safe_space_so/

PREMIERGARAGE. (2021, April 30). *Organizing sports equipment in a garage: A complete guide.* Premier Garage. https://www.premiergarage.com/blog/organizing-sports-equipment-in-a-garage-a-complete-guide/

Leesa. (n.d.). *Protect your bedroom at night: 5 Things that disrupt sleep.* https://www.leesa.com/article/5-ways-to-eliminate-bedroom-distractions

Pugle, M. (n.d.). *Executive function and ADHD: Symptoms and deficits.* Verywell Health. https://www.verywellhealth.com/executive-function-and-adhd-5210236

Pugle, M. (2022, March 11). *Distractibility or ADHD? How to tell the difference.* EverydayHealth.com. https://www.everydayhealth.com/adhd/are-you-simply-easily-distracted-or-do-you-have-adhd/

Rapson, S. (2021, July 14). *Reducing overwhelm with ADHD: Five steps to prioritise your tasks.* Unconventional Org. https://www.unconventionalorganisation.com/post/reducing-overwhelm-with-adhd-five-steps-to-prioritise-your-tasks

Redman, B. (2021, March 31). *Create a functional garage space for your DIY projects.* CaughtOnAWhim.com. https://caughtonawhim.com/diy-projects-garage-space/#google_vignette

Resnick, A. (2022). *What is executive dysfunction in ADHD?* Verywell Mind. https://www.verywellmind.com/what-is-executive-dysfunction-in-adhd-5213034

Rodden, J. (2017, February 17). *What Is executive dysfunction? Sign and symptoms of EFD.* ADDitude. https://www.additudemag.com/what-is-executive-function-disorder/

S, Maynard, y, & M.S. (2014, October 27). *6 Ways to build healthy new habits.* ADDitude. https://www.additudemag.com/healthy-habits-adult-adhd-focus/

Schatz, N. K., Aloe, A. M., Fabiano, G. A., Pelham, W. E., Smyth, A., Zhao, X., Merrill, B., Macphee, F., Ramos, M., Hong, N., & Altszuler, A. R. (2020). Psychosocial Interventions for Attention-Deficit/Hyperactivity Disorder: Systematic Review with Evidence and Gap Maps. *Journal of Developmental & Behavioral Pediatrics, 41*(2S), S77–S87. https://doi.org/10.1097/dbp.0000000000000778

Segal, R. (2019). *Managing Adult ADHD attention deficit disorder.* Help-

Guide.org. https://www.helpguide.org/articles/add-adhd/managing-adult-adhd-attention-deficit-disorder.htm

Shaw, P., Stringaris, A., Nigg, J., & Leibenluft, E. (2014). Emotion dysregulation in Attention Deficit Hyperactivity Disorder. *American Journal of Psychiatry, 171*(3), 276–293. https://doi.org/10.1176/appi.ajp.2013.13070966

Silk, T. J., Vance, A., Rinehart, N., Bradshaw, J. L., & Cunnington, R. (2009). White-matter abnormalities in attention deficit hyperactivity disorder: A diffusion tensor imaging study. *Human Brain Mapping, 30*(9), 2757–2765. https://doi.org/10.1002/hbm.20703

Smith, G. (2023). *Creating a sleep-friendly bedroom for ADHD children: Tips for establishing a sleep routine.* Woombie.com. https://woombie.com/blog/post/creating-a-sleep-friendly-bedroom-for-adhd-children-tips-for-estab lishing-a-sleep-routine-%7C-woombie

Team, T. M. (2020, February 20). *6 Expert tips for washing delicates.* The maids Blog. https://www.maids.com/blog/6-expert-tips-for-washing-delicates/

*The importance of organization - Escoffier.* (2017, December 18). Escoffier. https://www.escoffier.edu/blog/baking-pastry/the-importance-of-organization/

The Understood Team. (n.d.). *How Michael Phelps' ADHD helped him make olympic history.* Www.understood.org. https://www.understood.org/en/articles/celebrity-spotlight-how-michael-phelps-adhd-helped-him-make-olympic-history

*10 Daily bathroom cleaning habits.* (2017, May 27). One Happy Housewife. https://www.onehappyhousewife.com/bathroom-cleaning-habits/

*13: organizing your garage.* (n.d.). Take Control ADHD. https://takecontro ladhd.com/podcast/13

Tourjman, V., Louis-Nascan, G., Ahmed, G., DuBow, A., Côté, H., Daly, N., Daoud, G., Espinet, S., Flood, J., Gagnier-Marandola, E., Gignac, M., Graziosi, G., Mansuri, Z., & Sadek, J. (2022). Psychosocial Interventions for Attention Deficit/Hyperactivity Disorder: A Systematic Review and Meta-Analysis by the CADDRA Guidelines Work GROUP. *Brain Sciences, 12*(8), 1023. https://doi.org/10.3390/brainsci12081023

W, P. (2018, May 13). *Garage organization ideas for seasonal items.* SafeRacks. https://saferacks.com/blogs/organization-help/garage-organization-ideas-for-seasonal-items-2

Wall, F. (2021, February 14). *13 Tips & tricks for home camping gear storage.*

Flow Wall. https://www.flowwall.com/blog/13-tips-tricks-for-camping-gear-storage-at-home

Walsh, A. C. last updated C. from H. (2022, January 19). *How to plan a bathroom – a step-by-step guide to ensure your dream space.* Ideal Home. https://www.idealhome.co.uk/bathroom/bathroom-advice/planning-a-bathroom-190893

Washington, N. (2021, August 14). *ADHD and memory: Effects, tips, treatment & more.* Healthline. https://www.healthline.com/health/adhd/adhd-memory#memory-loss

Wetherspoon, D. (2021, May 3). *Sleeping with your TV on: Pros and cons.* Healthline. https://www.healthline.com/health/sleep/sleeping-with-tv-on#bottom-line

*When bad things happen to good kitchens (and how to avoid them when remodeling).* (n.d.). Apartment Therapy. https://www.apartmenttherapy.com/common-kitchen-design-pain-points-and-how-to-avoid-them-248923

*Why it's important that you keep your home organized.* (2021, August 3). Build Magazine. https://www.build-review.com/why-its-important-that-you-keep-your-home-organized/

Williams, S. (2019). *Self-Awareness and personal development.* Wright.edu. http://www.wright.edu/~scott.williams/LeaderLetter/selfawareness.htm

writer, staff. (2022, March 17). *How to organize office supplies like a professional.* Luce Blog. Sg.lucemg.com. https://sg.lucemg.com/blogs-articles/how-to-organize-office-supplies

Zito, B. (2015, December 11). *7 time management tips for cleaning your house.* Angi. https://www.angi.com/articles/time-management-strategies-clean-house.htm

Made in United States
Troutdale, OR
10/03/2024